SUPER EAGLES OF NIGERIA IN THE NEW ERA(2014-2018).
TABLE OF CONTENTS:

THE AUTHOR

Cyril Chukwudozie Nwokeji, is a Nigerian-born, Belgian-trained
Biotechnologist; a field in which he holds the Master's degree- M.Sc, from
the Vrije Universiteit Brussel. He also holds Bachelor's degrees in Nursing
Sciences, from the University College Leuven, Belgium and in Zoology,
from the University of Ilorin, Nigeria. He is married to Ann, and the couple
are blessed with three children. He presently lives and works in Belgium.
The author, has always been a very avid soccer enthusiast right from his
boyhood days. He played soccer for his class teams right up to his
secondary school days. During the orientation programme of the
compulsory National youth service corps programme: N.Y.S.C., in his
native country, Nigeria, the author, represented his platoon in soccer and
they won the "Inter-platoon soccer competition", at the N.Y.S.C.
orientation camp, in Uyo, in the then Cross-river state, in 1986.
This was the extent to which he went as an active soccer player; but his
interest in soccer only grew by leap and bounds, this time as a non-playing
soccer enthusiast and analyst. He has a non-rivalled passion for the game
of soccer; and, particularly, a very special interest in his country's senior
national soccer team: the Super Eagles of Nigeria. The author has keenly
followed the evolution of the Super Eagles from 1976 till date. He has met
and discussed with some former members of the Super Eagles; and has
spared no write-up in any news magazine, he can lay his hands on, on the
Super Eagles of Nigeria.

The author, also makes his contributions on soccer, more especially with regards the performances of the country's national teams, on the "Nigeria World forum."
Needless saying the author sees potential world-beaters in the Super Eagles, considering the huge abundance of talent, in his native country, Nigeria; on the condition that soccer administration is got right!
On the eve of what the author considers to be Nigeria's Super Eagles' rise to world soccer stardom, he has decided to put pen on paper, to give an account of how he has seen this gradual evolution/revolution take place since 1976. The book makes for interesting reading.

FOREWORD
When my friend of thirty years, whom I refer to as my brother from another mother, Cyril Nwokeji, asked me to write the foreword of his second book : " SUPER EAGLES OF NIGERIA IN THE NEW ERA", I didn't hesitate to say a capital yes! This was not only borne out of a desire to be of help to a long time bosom friend, but more especially, to give yearning to his crave/ passion for the beautiful round leather game: soccer. That Cyril loves the game of soccer, is actually an understatement, he craves for it; he is very passionate about it! It's like second nature to him!
And as a patriotic Nigerian, his 'first love' in this direction, is Nigeria's senior men's national team: the Super Eagles of Nigeria.
I can attest to the fact he has followed the evolution of this team for a very long time. When we first met in 1991, I noticed his passion not only for soccer, but specifically for the Super Eagles of Nigeria. He told me this special interest in the Super Eagles dates back to 1976, when he was only eleven years old!
The second book of his: "SUPER EAGLES OF NIGERIA IN THE NEW ERA", is actually a sequel to his first: "SUPER EAGLES OF NIGERIA: PRIDE OF AFRICA". Both books in my considered opinion are block- busters, that have, as never before, given a detailed insight into the Super Eagles of Nigeria, and it's significance to Nigerians. Without exaggerating the facts, one can describe them as the "twin bible of Nigerian football"! While the first book details how the Super Eagles have become the " Nigerian people's movement", the second book, " SUPER EAGLES OF NIGERIA IN THE NEW ERA," details how the Super Eagles of Nigeria, have grappled with the huge expectations of Nigerians as a consequence of its significance to them. And gives a verdict on how the Super Eagles have succeeded or not in meeting the Nigerian people's and other Super Eagles' supporters' huge expectations.
It's certainly a thriller waiting to be discovered!

Dr. Anthony Oluwole Ojo
A UK-based medical practitioner.

CHAPTER 1
INTRODUCTION

The author in the first book titled: "Super Eagles of Nigeria: Pride of Africa," told the story of how the Super Eagles of Nigeria have evolved to be not just another national soccer side, but "a peoples' movement," specifically, the "Nigerian peoples' movement." A team that all Nigerians identify with. A team that signifies the hope and aspirations of the Nigerian people. A team that signifies the promise of a better, united and more prosperous Nigeria!

In the second book: "Super Eagles of Nigeria in the New Era," the author narrates how the new status of the Super Eagles – "the Nigerian peoples movement"- has consequently placed huge expectations on the team, by Nigeria and Nigerians. The critical question at this juncture is: Will the Super Eagles of Nigeria, meet these huge expectations of Nigeria and Nigerians, in the new era?

In this book, the author, attempts to answer this critical question; which answer will certainly go a long way towards determining how Nigerians view the Super Eagles and the concomitant consequences for the image of the team as the Nigerian peoples' movement.

The author in his characteristic style, uses examples of matches played by the Super Eagles of Nigeria, in the aforementioned period, to make his case.

CHAPTER 2

THE IMMEDIATE AFTERMATH OF THE 2014 WORLD CUP COMPETITION

The end of the 2014 World cup competition, brought about many stark realities about the Super Eagles and the administration of soccer generally in Nigeria!

Firstly, the Super Eagles of Nigeria, had what in the eyes of observers, was a very average performance. It was generally believed the Super Eagles could have done better given the talent pool available to it. Soccer commentators blamed the very average performance of the team, on what they described as " the questionable World cup selection of Super Eagles' players". They believed that some good Nigerian players, were left out of the team purely for non-footballing/subjective reasons!

They gave the example of a Nigerian striker who plied his trade in the Spanish first division, who in the season 2013/2014, was the most prolific Nigerian striker in the whole of the European league, but was surprisingly left out of the team! This was despite the pressure put on the Nigerian coach by the media to take the facts into consideration before excluding the striker. The affected striker was reported to have phoned the Nigerian coach, before the 2014 World cup competition, and not only made up to him, for their so called differences, but also told the coach of his determination to do well for his country if selected for the World cup competition.

Despite these entreaties from the media and the player in question, the coach stubbornly left the top striker out of his World cup selection!

At the 2014 World cup competition, the Super Eagles of Nigeria, had difficulties scoring goals. They even played a scandalous goalless draw against soccer minnows Iran. A match Nigerians and soccer observers expected the Super Eagles to have easily won, given the relative strengths of both sides.

In the remaining 2014 World cup matches, the Super Eagles of Nigeria, had difficulties finding the back of the net! They managed three goals in four matches! An average of less than a goal a match! For a Super Eagles' team renowned for its offensive capabilities, this was scandalous!

Secondly, on the part of the soccer administrators, they were not without blame. The Super Eagles' players were reported to have missed a training session while preparing for the match against France, in the second round stage of the World cup competition. This was as a result of disagreement with the Nigerian Football Federation : N.F.F. , apparently, over non-payment of what was due the players.

The players were reported to have threatened to boycott the match against France, if their demands were not fully met.

The then Federal government, not wanting to be embarrassed at the world stage, reportedly, flew in money from Nigeria to the players. This money was shared between the players up to the wee hours of the day of the match with the French! Is it surprising the Super Eagles players who hitherto put up a strong resistance against the French, for the first seventy-five minutes of the match, fizzled out in the last fifteen minutes of the game?

On arrival back in Nigeria, after the World cup competition, the Federal government somewhat 'interfered' with the NFF's activities, when they 'prevailed' on the then NFF chairman, not to seek re-election.

This created a vacuum that opened the floodgates for all those who wanted to be NFF chairman – both the qualified and non-qualified soccer administrators- to throw their hats into the ring to fight for the NFF Chairmanship!

The fight for the NFF chairmanship, was to say the least, unorganized, chaotic and out rightly unorthodox! There was one big chaos, at the helm of Nigeria's soccer body.

The author in an article in the Nigeria World forum, titled:" The confusion in the NFF is killing the Super Eagles,"
(https://nigeriaworld.com/articles/2014/Sep/012.html), warned of the dire consequences of having an NFF in turmoil for Nigerian soccer!

The Federation of International Football Associations- FIFA, threatened to ban Nigeria from all its organized competitions, for what they called "government's interference" in the organization of Nigerian soccer and the general acts of lawlessness that characterized the organization of the NFF's election.

The Confederation of African Football Associations: CAF, also warned Nigeria, of the consequences of having an NFF in turmoil. The then CAF president, Alhaji Issa Hayatou, even went as far as saying that if Nigeria, wasn't willing to continue to be part of the international soccer family, the country should indicate that so that the international soccer family would forget about Nigeria! He said the CAF had not gotten as much trouble from other member associations, as it did from Nigeria!

The FIFA did in fact ban Nigeria for some days when the NFF's crisis appeared unresolvable! However, the timely 'retracing' of the government's and the NFF's footsteps, prevented a prolonged ban of Nigeria by FIFA.
Finally, sanity was restored to the NFF, with the election of Mr. Amaju Pinnick, as the NFF's Chairman!

CHAPTER 3
THE SECOND ERA OF COACH STEPHEN KESHI + CONCLUSIONS

While the NFF's crisis was still raging, the hour of the next international engagement for the Super Eagles- the qualification series for the 2015 African Nations' cup competition- came, and the Super Eagles were by no means ready as there was no coach in place at that time!
 The NFF board under the then chairman: Alhaji Maigari, didn't extend Coach Keshi's contract. Under normal circumstances, Coach Keshi, wasn't supposed to coach the Super Eagles beyond the 2014 World cup competition. However, the turmoil in the NFF, occasioned by lack of leadership, at the NFF, created a vacuum. This resulted in the lack of a substantive coach for the Super Eagles of Nigeria. In the above-mentioned article in the Nigeria world forum, the author urged the NFF, to renew Coach Keshi's contract, based on his performance as coach of the Super Eagles of Nigeria!
Thus, while the opponents of the Super Eagles were busy fine-tuning their strategies, the Super Eagles had no substantive coach and, thus, had not even started preparations for the AFCON 2015 qualification matches!
At this time of uncertainty, the then sports minister: Dr. Tammy Danigogo, decided to help out Nigerian soccer, by reaching a temporary agreement with Coach Keshi, to be paid on a "match-per-match" basis, so the Super Eagles' preparations for the AFCON qualifiers could commence.
The Super Eagles were grouped together with:
Congo Brazaville; Sudan and South-Africa, for the 2015 AFCON qualifiers. Two teams from the group would qualify for AFCON 2015.
When the draws for the 2015 AFCON was made, shortly before the 2014 World cup competition, the then NFF Chairman, Alhaji Maigari, predicted that Nigeria would come out tops from their group. Given the relative strengths of the opposition, one understood the reasons for his optimism. However, reality proved otherwise, as we shall see shortly.

NIGERIA VERSUS CONGO-BRAZAVILLE, 6th OF SEPTEMBER, 2014, IN UYO, NIGERIA.
The Super Eagles of Nigeria, took on the national team of Congo-Brazaville, on the aforementioned date. As earlier stated, the preparations of the Super Eagles, going into this match, was by no means proper. It was a case of a hastily assembled team, going to do battle with a well-prepared underdog!

The French coach of Congo-Brazaville: Claude Leroy, watched the video tapes of the Super Eagles of Nigeria, at the 2014 World cup competition, twenty-five times, before the encounter with the Nigerians! This was at a time the Super Eagles had no coach in place; talk less of preparing for the match against Congo-Brazaville!
The shoddy preparations, were further worsened by the late arrival of some senior players of the team to the training camp of the Super Eagles of Nigeria, in Uyo. The Nigerian coach: Stephen Keshi, was certainly not amused at this gross act of indiscipline on the part of some senior players. He subsequently made his feelings known to the affected players. One of the senior players, reacted badly by even asking to be excluded from the team, if the coach didn't want him again! The 'storm' that could have ensued between the affected player and the coach was temporarily laid to rest mainly due to the maturity of the Super Eagles' coach.
However, the events that preceded the Super Eagles' match against Congo-Brazaville, bode an ominous sign of what the outcome would be. The match indeed didn't go well for Nigeria, as the Super Eagles were beaten 3-2, before the home crowd. It was an unexpected victory for Congo-Brazaville!
And the first loss on home soil by the Super Eagles, in fourteen years!

IN THE AFTERMATH OF THE UNLIKELY LOSS TO CONGO-BRAZAVILLE!
At the press conference that followed the match, the press made it clearly known to the Coach Stephen Keshi, that the loss to Congo-Brazaville, was unacceptable to Nigerians. Coach Keshi, retorted that this was a soccer game and could go either way!
Needless saying Nigerians were utterly disappointed at the Super Eagles' home loss, notwithstanding the ominous signs that preceded the match: the NFF's crisis and all the other problems the team faced!
Yours sincerely in an article written on the Nigerian world forum titled :"A shocking home defeat to Congo Brazaville: The logical consequence of a confused NFF,"(https://nigeriaworld.com/articles/2014/sep/081.html), thought the loss was deserved, considering the foregoing!
The Super Eagles, thus, had a tall order, to rectify things against South-Africa, their next opponents!

NIGERIA VERSUS SOUTH-AFRICA, 10th OF SEPTEMBER, 2014, IN CAPE TOWN, SOUTH-AFRICA.
The Super Eagles' next port of call, was South-Africa, for the second match of the 2015 Nations' cup qualification series.
Nigeria needed to win the match to be on course for qualification from their group.
However, a goalless draw outing was the consequence of their encounter with South-Africa.
Thus, in two encounters, out of a possible six points, the Super Eagles garnered just one point! This was dismal considering Nigeria's status in African soccer.

NIGERIA VERSUS SUDAN, 11TH OCTOBER, 2014, IN KHARTUM, SUDAN.

The Super Eagles next port of call, was Khartoum, Sudan, for the continuation of the qualifying series for AFCON 2015. The Super Eagles were under tremendous pressure to win, to safe guard their qualification from the group.

On match day, the Super Eagles met a stuggy Sudanese team that gave them no quarters! They struggled to find their feet. It was clear this Sudanese team was a far better team than the Sudanese team mauled by the Super Eagles, 4-0, in 2001, in Khartoum, for the 2002 World cup qualifier!

The first half ended scoreless. Yours sincerely at that juncture, wondered if the Super Eagles of Nigeria, were equal to the task, with regards their objective, going into the match.

In the second half, there was no improvement in the performance of the Super Eagles of Nigeria. Rather we saw a Sudanese team that gradually took over control of the game.

It was a question of time before the Super Eagles caved in. Indeed, they did cave in, when as a consequence of some amateurish defending on the part of the central defenders: Godfrey Obo"fantastic" Abona and "Field Marshall" Kenneth Omeruo, a Sudanese attacker headed home the lone and winning goal, for the Sudanese team.

The score of Nigeria 0, Sudan 1, even in Khartoum, was an unlikely one! When the camera, focused on the Nigerian Coach: Stephen Keshi, his non-expressed behavior, or rather body language, showed a man who was somewhat dumbfounded at what was happening: the unlikely and unexpected likely loss to the Sudanese National team!

Indeed at the end of ninety minutes, the Super Eagles of Nigeria, lost to the Sudanese, 1-0; to garner just one point out of a likely nine points! Yours sincerely thought that loss would likely signal the end of Coach Keshi's reign as Super Eagles' coach!

THE AFTERMATH OF THE ENCOUNTER AGAINST THE SUDANESE, IN KHARTOUM.

Coach Keshi, apparently, wanting to starve off any attempt to sack him by the NFF, put out a statement in the press, in which he on behalf of the team, apologized for the unexpected loss to the Sudanese; and promised to rectify matters, in the return leg in Abuja; which took place four days after the first leg encounter.

This 'tactical' move, might indeed have staved off the immediate sacking of Coach Keshi; but just temporarily, with benefit of hindsight!

The Nigerian commentators severely criticized the team's performance. Some of them criticized the coach, for what they termed his constantly "rebuilding" the team, with new and in their eyes, players unfit for the national team of Nigeria! Some of them criticized the players, more especially the defenders, for defending like "amateurs!"

The die was thus cast for the return leg in Abuja, Nigeria, in a "must" win match for the Super Eagles of Nigeria!

NIGERIA VERSUS SUDAN, 15TH OCTOBER, 2014, IN ABUJA, NIGERIA.

The Super Eagles faced the Sudanese national team in the return leg, in Abuja, Nigeria. It was clear going into this match, the Super Eagles, had no choice but to win; if for nothing else to improve chances of qualification for AFCON 2015, and also to save the "head" of Coach Keshi!
The highly determined Super Eagles of Nigeria went after the Sudanese from the blast of the whistle. And pressurized them! The Sudanese initially defended with man and might, trying to contain the Super Eagles' offensive onslaught. They held out well in the first half; as the first half ended scoreless.
The score of Nigeria 0, Sudan 0, at half time, was unbelievable! At that juncture, a section of the home crowd lost their cool and started throwing bottled water in the direction of the players and the coaches! They openly demanded the sacking of Coach Keshi, through placards!
In the second half, the Super Eagles knew what they had to do to avoid the 'hell' Abuja, was likely to be to them!
They went out against the Sudanese in the second half and pinned them down to their half of the field, probing for openings through their compact defense. They eventually found them, as Ahmed Musa, in the 47th minute, capitalized on a defence-splitting pass from John Obi Mikel, to cleverly evade the Sudanese defenders and scored the first goal for Nigeria! The cheers that greeted this goal was deafening, as the fans cheered wildly! They apparently, temporarily, forget their anger at Coach Keshi and the team.
However, as a consequence of the usual lapses in the Super Eagles defence, the Sudanese capitalized on it to score the equalizer, against Nigeria, in the 54th minute! The Sudanese themselves couldn't believe their luck. They rejoiced excitedly!
The Super Eagles, knowing they still had to win, went after the Sudanese once again. They were eventually rewarded in the 65th and 89th minutes, through two goals scored by Aaron Samuel and Ahmed Musa, respectively, to bring the final scores to 3-1, in favour of Nigeria.
 The victory came with the concomitant three points for Nigeria! This hard fought out victory, increased the chances of qualification for AFCON 2015, for the Super Eagles of Nigeria.

THE DAY AFTER THE MATCH AGAINST THE SUDANESE, IN ABUJA.
The author thought a 3-1, victory, would soothe frayed Nigerian nerves, and in the meantime, save the job of Coach Keshi. But one was in for a rude shock, as the NFF, after an emergency meeting after the Sudanese encounter in Abuja, decided to sack Coach Keshi, and replaced him, on interim basis, with Coach Amodu Shaibu.
The NFF sited diminishing returns in the fortunes of the Super Eagles, in recent matches; and also the need to protect Coach Keshi, from irate soccer fans who could hurt him, if he continued coaching the Super Eagles. The NFF, claimed Coach Keshi, the hitherto popular coach, was no longer wanted by majority of Nigeria's soccer fans; no thanks to the then dwindling fortunes of the Super Eagles of Nigeria !

The author in an article in the Nigerian world forum titled : "Good bye to the 'big boss'," (https://nigeriaworld.com/articles/2014/oct/191.html), expressed his agreement with the decision of the NFF. The author will digress more on this, in the conclusions on this chapter.

Coach Amodu Shaibu, formally, started his tenure, by talking of how he was going to defeat Congo Brazaville, in the return leg, in Point Noire. He talked of his intentions to hit Congo Brazaville, "hard", at home!

However, in a surprising volte face, Coach Shaibu, now talked of his inability to take up coaching responsibility for the Super Eagles of Nigeria. He cited health reasons.

Later, it was learnt that the then Federal government, had intervened and wanted Coach Keshi re-instated!

When Coach Keshi, was cornered by news men and asked to comment on his re-instatement, he asked the rhetorical question: " If the President of Nigeria wanted me back on the job, who am I to refuse?" With Keshi's rhetorical question, it was clear, the 'deal' to get him back on the job, was already done!

Thus, Coach Keshi had to continue with the Super Eagles AFCON 2015 qualification series.

The author having analysed the Super Eagles' problems in recent times, wanted to write an article titled: " The need to strengthen the Super Eagles of Nigeria", but constraints of time prevented the author from doing it before the hour of the next international engagement came calling in Point Noire, Congo Brazaville.

Yours sincerely thought of writing the article, in response to what one saw was a gradual weakening of the Super Eagles, through introduction of weaker players into the team, in the rebuilding process of the team. This will be discussed in more detail in the conclusions to this chapter.

NIGERIA VERSUS CONGO BRAZAVILLE, 15TH NOVEMBER, 2014.

This was a match the Super Eagles had to win, and win by at least a two-goal margin, to stand a chance of qualification for the 2015 AFCON competition.

The chips were thus down for a helluvah fight against a home team that would fight to protect its prestige at home.

The match started with the Super Eagles trying to dictate the pace of the game, but all to no avail, as the home side held their own strongly, and even tried hitting back on some occasions. The match soon degenerated to a ding-dong affair, with no side clearly in control.

The first half, logically, ended scoreless.

In the second half, the Super Eagles intensified pressure on the home team. As a consequence, the home team conceded a penalty, which was converted by striker: Ike Uche, for Nigeria's first goal!

Congo Brazaville, fought back and also earned a penalty, which was missed!

The score, thus, remained 1-0, in favor of Nigeria.

The game appeared destined for a lone goal victory for Nigeria, until the 92nd minute, when Aaron Samuel, scored the vital second goal for Nigeria!

The Super Eagles, thus, won the match: 2-0, and collected all three points at stake!

THE DAY AFTER THE MATCH AGAINST CONGO BRAZAVILLE
Nigerians were happy and somewhat relieved the Super Eagles were a victory away from qualification for AFCON 2015. They were confident this victory would be gotten against South-Africa, in Nigeria.
In my preview of the match with a friend, one expressed his optimism at the possibility of qualification at home against South-Africa. The author's friend cautioned the author on the need to be careful and not to underrate the South-Africans. He was dead right, with benefit of hindsight.

NIGERIA VERSUS SOUTH-AFRICA, 19TH NOVEMBER, 2014.
The Super Eagles of Nigeria, took on the "Bafana-Bafana" of South-Africa, in Uyo, Nigeria on the aforementioned date.
The Super Eagles of Nigeria, looked destined to qualify for the 2015 AFCON tournament, considering the fact they needed a victory, regardless of the score line, against a beatable opponent on home soil.
They confidently went for this victory from the blast of the whistle. They created myriad of chances which were not utilized. This would later on hunt the Super Eagles, with benefit of hindsight.
The South-Africans occasionally countered, to send a notice that they would not be beaten easily. In a fortuitous South-African counter attack, the South-Africans scored in the 42nd minute, off a solo run into the Nigerian defense, by a South-African attacker. They led 1-0; the Nigerians reacted by piling more pressure on the South-Africans, but to no avail.
In the 48th minute of the first half, they scored a second goal, off a beautiful counter-attack, that further exposed Nigeria's defensive frailties!
The score of Nigeria 0, South-Africa 2, at half time, was unimaginable on the part of the Nigerian supporters of the Super Eagles; more especially, on home soil for that matter!
In the second half, the Super Eagles came all out to look for the equalizer. The Nigerian coach made the necessary substitutions, and the Super Eagles piled more pressure on the South-Africans. But all to no avail. As the time ticked away, the South-Africans grew in confidence. It increasingly looked like the Super Eagles wouldn't be able to pull the chest nut out of the fire and qualify for AFCON 2015. They kept on coming, while the South-Africans defended ruggedly, closing out all the spaces to the Super Eagles. But the Super Eagles were determined to survive.
 In one of their moves into the South-African territory, a powerful shot taken by a Super Eagles player, was blocked on to the path of another Super Eagles player, by the South-African goalkeeper. This gift was taken by the Super Eagles player- Sone Aluko- for Nigeria's first goal!
The score of Nigeria 1, South-Africa 2, encouraged the Nigerians, who probed deeper into the South-African territory for more goals.
The equalizer, came in the 95th minute, off a powerful shot taken by Sone Aluko, from about twenty-five meters!
The final score was: Nigeria 2, South-Africa 2.

The Super Eagles, thus, failed to qualify for the 2015 AFCON tournament, for the third time in Nigeria's soccer history!
Clearly, the Super Eagles, had tumbled to new lows, from their exalted position in the aftermath of the AFCON victory of 2013!

THE DAY AFTER THE FAILED QUALIFICATION FOR AFCON 2015
Nigerians were not amused, with this latest and unexpected set back in her soccer development. Coach Keshi, apparently, sensing the mood of the nation, chose not to attend the post-match press conference! He was certainly a coach under fire for the failed qualification for AFCON 2015.
Tongs started wagging about the reasons for Nigeria's failure. Some commentators blamed the failure on the NFF's crisis.
Others blamed Coach Keshi, for what they termed : "wrongful rebuilding process" of the Super Eagles of Nigeria.
An ex- Nigerian international soccer player, accused Coach Keshi, of constantly rebuilding the Super Eagles, as a consequence of "selfish interest" !
And yet others blamed the then new NFF chairman: Mr. Amaju Pinnick, for what they termed, "administrative incompetence!"
Regardless of the side of the aisle one belonged, one thing was clear: Nigerians were collectively angry at the failure of the Super Eagles to qualify for AFCON 2015!

CONCLUSIONS ON THE SECOND ERA OF COACH KESHI
Coach Keshi, certainly failed in his second coming –albeit- on a temporary basis as coach of the Super Eagles. This resulted in the failure of the Super Eagles to qualify for AFCON 2015. The failure of the team showed that the success gotten by Coach Keshi, at AFCON 2013, had all but disappeared! It was absolutely clear the Super Eagles of Nigeria, needed a new and thorough rebuilding process, under a coach to be determined by the NFF. We shall discuss this later on.
Why did Coach Keshi fail in his second coming?
Me thinks the following factors played a role:
1) The NFF crisis didn't help matters. At a time Nigeria needed to focus on the AFCON 2015 qualifiers, Nigeria was distracted by the governing body of soccer's crisis! This certainly hampered the Super Eagles' preparations.
2) The New NFF board that was finally put in place, didn't settle properly on the job, as a consequence of the NFF crisis. The board started its work later than normal. There was no time for proper transition, between the old and the new NFF boards.
3) The Super Eagles' coach, though hired on a temporary basis, made the mistake of rebuilding the 2014 World cup team with some players of questionable quality! Given the rising standards of African soccer, this proved to be 'fatal' !
4) Coach Keshi was apparently not motivated enough to work, considering the fact he was hired on a temporary basis, when he expected a longer term contract from the NFF. His motivation was apparently further dampened by his dismissal during the course of the qualifiers!

5) Coach Keshi, as a former defender, paradoxically, couldn't organize Nigeria's defense! This made the Super Eagles concede very cheap goals! Goals that sometimes made a difference with regards the overall result of a game.

As earlier stated, the Super Eagles as a consequence of failure for AFCON 2015, needed a thorough rebuilding. The question was which coach would do the job for Nigeria? Yours sincerely in an article titled: "AFCON 2015: A deserved failure for Nigeria!," (https://nigeriaworld.com/articles/2014/nov/240.html), in the Nigeria world forum, spoke out his preference for a foreign coach who would do the job for Nigeria.

One reasoned that since Coach Keshi had been in charge of the team, as at then, for three years, with the upside to his performance: the AFCON 2013 success and an ignominious downside: failure at AFCON 2015, Nigeria needed to move in a new direction!

With benefit of hindsight, the failure of the NFF to heed this piece of advice, proved to be costly for Nigeria, in the AFCON 2017 qualifiers, as we shall see later on.

CHAPTER 4
THE BRIEF THIRD ERA OF COACH STEPHEN KESHI + CONCLUSIONS

The third era of Coach Keshi, didn't start immediately. As a matter fact, in the immediate aftermath of Nigeria's failure to qualify for AFCON 2015, most soccer commentators, believed Coach Keshi, should leave the Super Eagles job. The "Big Boss" would have none of that. Despite persistent calls to resign, he dug in, and deep for that matter!

The NFF on other hand, who had the same feeling as most Nigerians –that Coach Keshi needed to resign- couldn't effectualize their expectations, as they were apparently afraid to move against Coach Keshi, fearing his connections to the highest places in the then Federal government!

The consequence was that the Super Eagles were without a substantive coach for many months! Valuable time was lost, that could have been utilized in the rebuilding process of the Super Eagles of Nigeria!

The author, seeing what was happening, wrote an article titled: " Whither NFF and the substantive Super Eagles' coach," (https://nigeriaworld.com/articles/2015/jan/181.html), in the Nigeria world forum, in which the author highlighted the consequences of time wasting in the rebuilding process of the Super Eagles of Nigeria.

The author's advice was not heeded and the Super Eagles were without a substantive coach for some months.

The unenviable situation of the Super Eagles notwithstanding, the time for the next international engagement came, and the Super Eagles had to be represented.

The Super Eagles played two friendly matches in January 2015: against Kuwait; The Super Eagles defeated Kuwait, 2-0, in Kuwait city.

The Super Eagles next played the national team of Cote D' Ivoire =(Ivory Coast), on the 11th of January, 2015. The Ivorians narrowly defeated the Super Eagles, 1-0; courtesy of an 84th minute goal, scored by Salomon Kalou. The Super Eagles were reported to have put up a good performance, with a team of mainly fringe players, who played against one of the then best teams in Africa; that went ahead and won the 2015 AFCON competition!

The Super Eagles were coached in the aforementioned matches by the technical crew led by the stand-in coach: Daniel Amokachi.

The Super Eagles of Nigeria, on the 25th of March, 2015, took on the Uganda national team, the "Cranes", in a friendly encounter, that also signaled the formal opening of the "Godswill Akpabio International stadium," Uyo! The "Cranes" spoilt the party, when they ran away with a 1-0 victory, against a very weak Super Eagles team!

The Super Eagles performance was so dismal that the NFF Chairman, angrily spoke to the players, and charged them to be up and doing for Nigeria!

That match also signaled the break-up of the working relationship between Coach Amokachi and Coach Keshi. This was as a result of the comments credited to Coach Amokachi, in which he said that Coach Keshi –from behind the scenes- selected the team that lost to Uganda. Coach Keshi, who then was rounding up negotiations with the NFF, for a new contract, immediately, signaled the end of the working relationship with Coach Amokachi!

The Super Eagles of Nigeria, next took on the South-African team on the 29th March, 2015, in South-Africa. The then Coach Daniel Amokachi-tutored side, scored an 85th minute goal, through Ahmed Musa, that looked like the winner; but the South-Africans got a 93rd minute equalizer, to end the match at 1-1 apiece

In that match, the Nigerian goalkeeper: Daniel Akpeyi, was so good that a South-African team: "Chippa United," signed him on!

Finally in April 2015, the "ice" was broken, the NFF reached an agreement with Coach Keshi, for a new two year contract; this was subsequently signed by the two parties!

THE 2017 NATIONS' CUP (AFCON) QUALIFIERS

The Super Eagles of Nigeria were grouped alongside: Egypt; Chad and Tanzania, for the 2017 Nations' cup qualifiers.

Only one team, would qualify from the group! Thus, it was clear from the onset that the Super Eagles of Nigeria, were in for a fight, considering the quality of the opposition; particularly Egypt!

However, for the Nigerian supporters of the Super Eagles of Nigeria, only the best was good enough- qualification for AFCON 2017; anything else was unacceptable!

Coach Keshi, thus, had a herculean task to raise a Super Eagles team that would rise up to the occasion in these circumstances.

Coach Keshi told the press that he needed to completely rebuild the Super Eagles, since the 2013 AFCON-winning team was no more in place. This certainly made the task much more difficult.

However, in a rather optimistic tone, Coach Keshi expressed his faith and belief in the Super Eagles' capability of winning the African Nations' cup competition again!

NIGERIA VERSUS CHAD, 13th JUNE, 2015.
In the days leading up to this encounter, the skipper of the Super Eagles, Goalkeeper Vincent Enyeama, spoke his concerns out to the press, about the safety of Kaduna, as venue of the match, apparently, in the light of the security challenges then facing the nation.
 These remarks were certainly not appreciated by the NFF, who subsequently called skipper Enyeama to order!
Coach Keshi used the opportunity of the encounter against the Chadians, to 'launch' the new- look Super Eagles ; made up of mainly new players. The following players lined-up for Nigeria:
Goalkeeper and Skipper Vincent Enyeama was in goal. The Defenders were: Leon Balogun, at right back; Kingsley Madu (a debutant), at left back; William Troost-Ekong (a debutant), at centre-half back and Kenneth Omeruo, at left-half back.
Thus, the defence had two new defenders who played for the first time for Nigeria (= the debutants!)
The mid-field was reorganized, there was no place for John Mikel Obi! The playmaker's role fell to :Babatunde Michael. The other mid-fielders were the defensive mid-fielders: Ogenyi Onazi and John Ogu.
The offensive front was also re-orgnaised: Ahmed Musa, was the right winger; Gbolahan Salami, was the left winger; while Aaron Samuel, was the centre-forward.
The team played in a 4-3-3 formation.
They took the initiative from the kick off, and pressurized the Chadians.
The Chadians defended strongly, denying the Super Eagles every inch of space. They held on strongly till the end of the first half, which was scoreless.
In the second half, the Super Eagles, intensified their pressure on the Chadians.
The injured Aaron Samuel was replaced by Odion Ighalo. In the 62nd minute, a one-two combination between the Super Eagles' players close to the Chadian penalty box, saw Gbolahan Salami, liberated with a pass from Ogenyi Onazi, in the Chadian penalty box, he took his opportunity with both hands as he fired home from close range for Nigeria's first goal!
It was thus: Nigeria1, Chad 0.
In the 78th minute, Odion Ighalo, was wrestled down to the ground by a Chadian defender, in the Chadian penalty box! The resultant penalty kick was converted by Odion Ighalo, for Nigeria's second goal.
Nigeria, thus, won, 2-0, to collect the three points at stake; and, thus, made a fairly good start to their AFCON 2017 qualification battle, based on their points advantage.

THE AFTERMATH OF THE ENCOUNTER AGAINST THE CHADIANS

The performance of the Super Eagles, was to say the least unimpressive!
The Nigerian press grilled Coach Keshi, in this regard. Coach Keshi,
answered by pointing out to the press that he was building a new team,
and Nigerians needed to be patient with him. He told the press that in
subsequent matches, he would introduce more of the new players.
The NFF, in a new development, queried Coach Keshi over the presence in
the team (on the substitute's bench) of a player that played in the third
division of the Nigerian league! The NFF, wondered what criteria were used
by Coach Keshi, for the invitation of players to the Super Eagles!
However, due to unforeseen events, Coach Keshi, could not answer to this
query, as we shall soon see.

THE SACKING OF COACH KESHI
The nation woke up to the surprising, but certainly not unwanted sacking
of Coach Keshi, by the NFF!
The official explanation was that Coach Keshi violated the terms of his
contract by applying for the job of national coach of Ivory Coast, without
permission from his employers, the NFF.
The NFF saw his name on the internet, as one of those coaches who
applied to coach the Ivorian national team; and promptly sacked him!
The author thinks the sacking of Coach Keshi, was more a case of an NFF,
that saw a chance to do away with an unwanted coach, who was imposed
on them by circumstances, than the so called reason given for his
dismissal. If Coach Keshi, had committed that so-called offence when the
administration of Dr. Goodluck Jonathan was in power, would he have
been botted out?
Anyhow, Coach Keshi's exit paved the way for the reorganization and re-
positioning of the Super Eagles. This step should have been taken almost
one year earlier, if not for the sometimes lackadaisical way of
administering Nigerian soccer! The inability to do the right thing at the
right time in this regard, proved to be costly for Nigeria, for the 2017
AFCON qualifiers, as we shall see.

POST MORTEM ANALYSIS
The third coming of Coach Keshi, was too short for a post-mortem
analysis.
However, the author holds strongly to the views expressed in the
"Conclusions", on Coach Keshi's second coming as coach.
The author supported the re-appointment of Coach Keshi, as Super Eagles'
coach, in the immediate aftermath of the 2014 World cup competition. But
made a volte face when the author saw the way and manner Coach Keshi
went about his job- albeit on a temporary basis. The NFF board that came
on board after the NFF's crisis, shirked their responsibility with regards
Coach Keshi, when it was clear he didn't deserve to be Super Eagles' coach
anymore; for earlier mentioned reasons. Nigeria paid a big price for the
apparent dereliction of responsibility by the NFF!
In other words, Coach Keshi, was sacked rather belatedly, by the NFF!

CHAPTER 5

THE ERA OF COACH SUNDAY OLISEH + CONCLUSIONS

The sacking of Coach Keshi necessitated the appointment of a new
substantive coach! In my article titled " AFCON 2015: A deserved failure
for Nigeria !",(https://nigeriaworld.com/articles/2014/nov/240.html), on
the "Nigeria world forum", yours sincerely made a case for the
employment of a foreign coach, as the Super Eagles' coach.
Apparently, the NFF, were on the same page with the author; but when
this construction, was presented to Coach Oliseh, in which he would assist
the foreign coach, he apparently, flatly rejected it. Preferring instead to be
Super Eagles' substantive coach.
This wish was acceded to by the NFF, who appointed him Super Eagles'
substantive coach.
The author in an article in the "Nigeria world forum", notwithstanding the
fact Coach Oliseh was not the author's first choice as coach of the Super
Eagles, nonetheless, supported the NFF's choice, through the article:"
Welcome Coach Sunday Oliseh",
(https://nigeriaworld.com/articles/2015/jul/231.html).
 The NFF Chairman: Mr. Amaju Pinnick, in confirming the choice of Coach
Oliseh, expressed the hope that notwithstanding his relative lack of
experience, would turn out to be another Coach Pep Guardiola – the
former FC Barcelona coach, who was so successful, notwithstanding his
relative lack of experience as coach, as at the time he took over the
coaching responsibility of FC Barcelona!
 Coach Sunday Oliseh's choice was generally well received by Nigerians. He
was enthusiastically welcomed by the usually soccer-crazy Nigerians on
arrival at the " Nnamdi Azikiwe" International Airport, Abuja.
At his first press conference, in Abuja, he promised more than hundred
percent effort, in the rebuilding of the Super Eagles of Nigeria, but couldn't
promise hundred percent success!
Thus, Coach Oliseh started his work as Super Eagles' coach with the very
best of goodwill from the usually demanding Nigerians; who are usually
very passionate about their dear Super Eagles of Nigeria.

NIGERIA VERSUS TANZANIA, 5th SEPTEMBER, 2015
Coach Oliseh's first challenge was a 2017 Nations' cup qualifier, away, in
Dar Es salaam, against Tanzania. It was Nigeria's second match in the
qualification series for AFCON 2017.
In his first press conference, Coach Sunday Oliseh, caused quite a stir,
when he said only players from first division teams would be invited to the
Super Eagles. He later on retraced his footsteps when the press convinced
him of the unrealisability of his intentions.
In the build-up to this encounter, Coach Sunday Oliseh, called-up the best
Nigerian soccer players, mainly professional players who plied their trade
in foreign countries.
The press as usual sat virtually on his throat at this time. He was
constantly grilled by the press about the chances of the Super Eagles
against a supposedly weak team of the group. He did his best to answer
them to the best of his ability.

However, at one occasion, in the hours leading up to the encounter, when the journalists once again wanted to know the chances of Nigeria against Tanzania; he retorted that in any soccer game, there were three possibilities: a win; a defeat or a draw! With this response the press got the message that Coach Oliseh wanted to be left alone to focus fully on the match.

Indeed total focus was needed not only by the coach, but also by the players, as they met a highly determined Tanzanian team ready to do battle against the Super Eagles! The Tanzanians urged on by their supporters, took on the Super Eagles of Nigeria, without complexes.

They out-played the Super Eagles for the entire duration of the match; they created a myriad of chances which a combination of inexperience on the part of their players; an excellent goalkeeper Carl Ikeme; and sheer luck on the part of the Super Eagles, prevented them from utilizing to have gotten what would have been a well -deserved victory!

Goalkeeper Carl Ikeme, in his very first match for the Super Eagles, instantly, became the star of the team; he was the man of the match! Goalkeeper Carl Ikeme, fortuitously stared for the Super Eagles in that match as last minute replacement for the then bereaved first choice goalkeeper: Skipper Vincent Enyeama.

The match against a supposedly weaker team, ended scoreless; paradoxically, to the great relief of Nigerians and all Super Eagles' supports who watched as the Super Eagles of Nigeria were out-played in all departments of the game by the supposedly weaker Tanzanians!

THE DAY AFTER THE MATCH AGAINST THE TANZANIANS
The Nigerian press expectedly descended heavily on the team, with scathing criticisms after their lack-luster performance against Tanzania. A Nigerian journalist, with benefit of hindsight, rightly predicted that the Super Eagles of Nigeria would not qualify for the AFCON 2017 competition! The author like some super-committed supporters of the Super Eagles, disagreed, and hoped for significant improvement on the part of the Super Eagles of Nigeria. We were to be disappointed later on.

Goalkeeper Carl Ikeme, when asked about the chances of the Super Eagles against Egypt, one of the Super Eagles' opponents in the group, said the Super Eagles needed to work harder to get the ticket to AFCON 2017.

Carl Ikeme, by his heroics, in the match, instantly became the star of the team, and made Nigerians to start thinking comfortably about 'life' without then skipper and goalkeeper Vincent Enyeama, who had earlier signaled that AFCON 2017,was to be his last tournament as a Super Eagle.

Coach Sunday Oliseh, thus, had a lot of work to do to get Nigerians the Super Eagles of their dreams!

NIGERIA VERSUS NIGER, 8TH SEPTEMBER, 2015.

The Super Eagles faced the national team of Niger, the "Menas", in a friendly encounter, in Port-Harcourt, on the aforementioned date. The Super Eagles erased the bad performance in Tanzania, a few days earlier, with a 2-0 victory. The goals came from an 11th minute penalty kick taken by Skipper Ahmed Musa, after Anthony Ujah was fouled in the penalty box of Niger; and an 85th minute goal scored by Simon Moses. To hand Coach Oliseh his first win as coach of the Super Eagles of Nigeria!

NIGERIA VERSUS DEMOCRATIC REPUBLIC OF CONGO, 8th OKTOBER, 2015.
The Super Eagles took on the Democratic Republic of Congo, in a friendly match, in Vise, Belgium. The match was geared towards preparing the team for the challenges ahead.
At the team's training camp, in Belgium, there was a fall-out between Coach Sunday Oliseh, and then Skipper Vincent Enyeama. It lead to the then Skipper Vincent Enyeama, prematurely, leaving the camp. He was later on called back, he came back, but apparently, as a consequence, decided to pre-maturely announce his retirement from the Super Eagles.
 Ahmed Musa, became the new skipper of the Super Eagles!
Apparently, as consequence of the above mentioned problem in the Super Eagles training camp, the Super Eagles were not focused enough in the match against the Democratic Republic of Congo.
The Super Eagles lost the match, 2-0, to their opponents!
The Super Eagles were thus under pressure to do well in their next friendly match against the Camerounians.

NIGERIA VERSUS CAMEROUN, 11TH OF OCTOBER,2015.
The Super Eagles took on the "Indomitable Lions" of Cameroun, in the second friendly match in the aforementioned month, in Molenbeek, Belgium. The author was one of the spectators that cheered the Super Eagles on that day.
 Coach Sunday Oliseh lined-up the following players:
Goalkeeper Carl Ikeme, was in goal. The Defenders were: Shehu Abdullahi, at right back; Elderson Echiejile, was at left back; Leon Balogun, was centre-half back; and Efe Ambrose, was left-half back.
The mid-fielders were: Ogenyi Onazi- defensive mid-field; John Mikel Obi- offensive mid-fielder; and Sylvester Igbonu- offensive mid-fielder.
The strikers were: Skipper Ahmed Musa, right winger; Simon Moses, left winger; and Emmanuel Emenike, centre-forward.
The Super Eagles played in an offensive 4-3-3 formation; and took the initiative from the blast of the referee's whistle. They dominated the game and were rewarded in the 39th minute, when Efe Ambrose connected with a glancing header a free-kick perfectly taken by John Mikel Obi, for Nigeria's first goal! The Super Eagles held on to their advantage at half time.

In the second half, the Super Eagles dominance continued and they were rewarded in the 61ˢᵗ minute, when in a brilliant counter-attack, Skipper Ahmed Musa, launched the onrushing Simon Moses with a nice cross- field pass, which he beautifully collected, expertly went past a Camerounian defender, before unleashing a powerful left-footed shot that sailed untouched into the Camerounian net for the second goal of Nigeria!
From then onwards, the Super Eagles controlled the game; and they scored a third goal through another glancing header from Odion Ighalo, off a beautiful pull out from Elderson Echiejile.
The Super Eagles won the match:3-0.

THE AFTERMATH OF THE ENCOUNTER AGAINST THE CAMEROUNIANS
Nigerians were happy at the result of the match.
 On the "Nigeria world forum", the author, in an article titled: "When the Super Eagles came to town !,"
(https://nigeriaworld.com/feature/publication/nwokeji/102415.html), expressed the hope, based on the performance of the Super Eagles, in a better tomorrow for the Super Eagles of Nigeria!
The match against the Camerounians, signaled the last match of Emmanuel Emenike for the Super Eagles of Nigeria; as he subsequently retired from international soccer!

NIGERIA VERSUS BURKINA-FASO, 17ᵀᴴ OCTOBER, 2015.
The home-based Super Eagles of Nigeria, faced the "Stallions" of Burkina-faso, in the final eliminator of the "African Nations' Championship" or the "CHAN" championship, to determine the qualifiers for the CHAN championship in Rwanda, in 2016.
The CHAN championship or tournament, is a national teams' tournament, for the home-based players of member nations of the "Confederation of African Football," or "CAF."
The Super Eagles defeated the "Stallions" of Burkina-Faso, 2-0,in the first leg match, in Port-harcourt, Nigeria.

NIGERIA VERSUS BURKINA-FASO, 25ᵀᴴ OCTOBER, 2015.
In the return leg in Ouagadougou, Burkina-faso, the Super Eagles without Coach Sunday Oliseh, who suddenly took ill, during preparations for the return leg, and, subsequently, had to fly back to his Belgian base, and coached by Coach Salisu Yusuf, played out a goalless draw against the "Stallions", in Ouagadogou.
The Super Eagles overcame great odds to qualify, including a penalty kick awarded Niger, which was saved by the Nigerian goalkeeper!
The home-based Super Eagles, thus, qualified on 2-0, goals aggregate, for the CHAN championship at the expense of Burkina-faso, to record the first major success for the Coach Sunday Oliseh-led technical crew!
The author, acknowledged this success in the "Nigeria world forum", with an article titled: " A first success for the Coach Sunday Oliseh-led technical crew !,"
(https://nigeriaworld.com/feature/publication/nwokeji/103015.html)

THE 2018 PRELIMINARY WORLD CUP QUALIFIER

The FIFA or Federation of International Football Associations, released a format for the 2018 World cup qualifiers, which entailed a preliminary knock-out round of matches, before the division of the survivors in five groups, where only the group's winners will emerge to represent Africa at the 2018 World cup competition.
The Super Eagles of Nigeria were drawn to meet Swaziland, in a two-legged knock-out match, to determine which team will advance to the group's stages of the elimination series.

NIGERIA VERSUS SWAZILAND, 13TH NOVEMBER, 2015.
The Super Eagles of Nigeria played out a goalless draw against Swaziland, in the first leg match in Swaziland. It was a match the Super Eagles dominated but could not find an opening into the tightly organized defensive formation of the Swazis.

THE RETURN LEG, 17TH NOVEMBER, 2015.
The Super Eagles encountered the "Sihlangu Semnikati" of Swaziland, in the return leg in Port-Harcourt, Nigeria. Going into the match, the Super Eagles were the favorites to win and qualify for the next stage of the World cup qualifiers. They were not only expected to win, they were expected to win big; by a monstrous score line! Nigerians were even disappointed the Super Eagles failed to win in Swaziland.
In the return leg, Coach Sunday Oliseh, took the unusual step of leaving John Mikel Obi, on the substitute's bench! This decision with benefit of hindsight, proved to be a wise one for two reasons:
1) The player that replaced him: Paul Onobi, was a capable replacement!;
2) The replacement of John Obi Mikel, tactically disorganized the Swazis! Their coach told reporters after the return match, that he tactically planned his game around stopping John Mikel, who based on proceedings from the first leg match, was the tactical lynch pin of Nigeria. He said the Nigerian coach really took him by surprise; a surprise that contributed to their loss to Nigeria.
The following players lined-up for Nigeria:
Goalkeeper Carl Ikeme, was in goal. The defenders were: Shehu Abdullahi, right full-back; Uche Okas, left full-back; Obaraokpo, centre-half back and Efe Ambrose, left-half back.
The mid-fielders were: Ogenyi Onazi, defensive mid-fielder; Paul Onobi, central/ defensive mid-fielder and Sylvester Igbonu, offensive mid-fielder.
The strikers were: Skipper Ahmed Musa, winger; Simon Moses, winger; Odion Ighalo, centre-forward.
The Super Eagles of Nigeria in their 4-3-3 formation, took the initiative from the blast of the referee's whistle and pressurized the Swazis. But all to no avail, as a lack of creativity on the part of the Nigerians prevented them from causing havoc in the vital area of the Swazis. This pattern of play continued till the end of the first half, which ended on a scoreless note.

In the second half, the Super Eagles, intensified their pressure on their opponents. This time around, they played the ball faster and changed positions on the field of play much more frequently. As a consequence, they gradually started finding openings in the defensive organization of the Swazis. But their brilliant goalkeeper prevented the Nigerians from scoring. However, in the 50th minute, the first of two free-kicks that re-defined the game in Nigeria's favor, was given, and Simon Moses, expertly converted the kick, for Nigeria's first goal! The Nigerian bench and Nigerians were greatly relieved.

In the 85th minute, another free-kick taken by Sylvester Igbonu, was brilliantly ticked into the net by the alert and brilliant, Efe Ambrose, for Nigeria's second and last goal!

The Super Eagles won the match, 2-0, to qualify for the group's stages of the 2018 World cup qualifiers.

THE DAY AFTER THE MATCH
 Some Nigerians in their sometimes unbridled arrogance, were not satisfied with the victory of the Super Eagles over Swaziland. They argued that a 2-0 score line, was not good enough as margin of victory over the Swazis, whom they considered a very weak team to the Super Eagles.

At the post-match press conference, some of the journalists were of the same opinion.

Coach Oliseh replied by saying that he would have been worried if the Super Eagles of Nigeria, didn't create chances during the match.

In an article on the "Nigeria world forum", titled: " A second success for the Coach Sunday Oliseh-led technical crew!," (https://nigeriaworld.com/feature/publication/nwokeji/120215.html), the author cautioned these Nigerians on the need to be humble and to recognize the fact that the standards of African soccer have risen over the years.

THE 2016 AFRICAN NATIONS' CHAMPIONSHIP(CHAN) IN RWANDA.
As earlier stated the "African Nations' championship" or "CHAN" championship, is a tournament for the home-based players of member countries of the "Confederation of African Football" or "CAF". The tournament like the "African Nations' cup" tournament is held bi-annually. At the 2016 edition of the competition, the Super Eagles of Nigeria(home-based), participated alongside sixteen other nations.

In an article by the author on the "Nigeria World forum", titled: "A first success for the Coach Sunday Oliseh-led technical crew!,"(https://nigeriaworld.com/feature/publication/nwokeji/103015.html), the author urged Coach Oliseh, to make the Super Eagles of Nigeria, African champions of the CHAN competition!

Nigerians also had this expectation and consequently mindset, when the CHAN competition started in Rwanda, in January, 2016.

The Super Eagles of Nigeria, were drawn in the same group with: Niger; Tunisia and Guinea.

NIGERIA VERSUS NIGER, JANUARY 18th, 2016.

The Super Eagles faced the national team of Niger, the "Menas", in their first match of the CHAN championship.
In the first half, the Super Eagles couldn't find a way through the tight defensive organization of Niger.
A frustrated Coach Oliseh, could be seen shouting instructions to the players from the sidelines, but to no avail.
In the second half, the Super Eagles found a way out of the 'quagmire', by scoring in the 45th, 73rd, 83rd and 92nd minutes of the game.
The Nigerians pulled one back, in the 80th minute.
The Super Eagles of Nigeria won the game, 4-1, to collect all three points at stake!
Chisom Chikatara, scored a hat-trick (three goals in the match)!

THE DAY AFTER THE MATCH
Nigerians were elated the first match was won convincingly. Nigerians, including the author, started dreaming of the Super Eagles' advancement beyond the preliminary rounds.

NIGERIA VERSUS TUNISIA, JANUARY 22nd 2016.
The Super Eagles of Nigeria next faced the Tunisian national team, "the Carthage Eagles", in the second match of the preliminary rounds.
After a goalless first half, the Super Eagles took the lead in the 52nd minute, through Chisom Chikatara.
The Tunisians levelled up in the 70th minute.
The two teams shared the points at one a piece; to keep hopes alive for an eventual qualification of the Super Eagles of Nigeria, for the knock-out series of the tournament.

NIGERIA VERSUS GUINEA, JANUARY 26TH , 2016.
The Super Eagles played their third and final match of the preliminary rounds, against the "Sylli Stars" of Guinea. The Super Eagles needed at least a draw to get into the next round: the knock-out phase of the competition.
The author like all Nigerians expected at the very least a draw from the Super Eagles, for advancement. We were all so sure of a good result and qualification for the next round!
However, we were awoken with the rude shock of the loss to the Guineans and the concomitant unlikely and highly unexpected elimination of the Super Eagles from the CHAN competition!
The Super Eagles of Nigeria, lost by the oddest of margins: 1-0, to the Guineans!

THE AFTERMATH OF THE UNLIKELY ELIMINATION OF THE SUPER EAGLES OF NIGERIA FROM THE CHAN COMPETITION
All hell was let loose as a consequence of the highly unexpected exit of the Super Eagles from the CHAN competition!
The press and public alike descended heavily on Coach Sunday Oliseh.
Nigerians like the poor losers they are, couldn't accept the defeat and early elimination from CHAN.

Soccer commentators questioned the suitability of Coach Oliseh for the Super Eagles' coaching job. Some of them questioned the procedure used in employing Coach Oliseh.
Others suggested the outright sacking of Coach Oliseh!
An NFF official even suggested the NFF would henceforth 'interfere' with Coach Oliseh's coaching responsibility and even suggested the possible screening of the players' list submitted by Coach Oliseh, in the future, by the NFF! In the words of the NFF official: " We won't let Coach Oliseh coach us to hell!"

COACH SUNDAY OLISEH'S UNPRECEDENTED REACTION!
Coach Oliseh on his part, apparently, took the criticisms to the chin, by putting out a video message in reaction to the myriad of criticisms he received as a consequence of the above-mentioned scenario.
In the video message, he took a swipe at his criticasters, by telling them Nigeria was not the only big name soccer nation, that didn't do well at the CHAN competition. He wondered why he was so 'badly' treated in the media, considering the relatively 'friendly' treatment gotten by the other coaches of the other big name soccer nations in Africa, who flopped at the CHAN competition.
He further talked of how some unpatriotic Nigerians had tried to induce him to do things in an unorthodox way as a way to make extra money on the job!
It was the first time in the history of Nigerian soccer that a coach of the Super Eagles would go that far: releasing a video message, to reply his critics!

THE NFF'S REACTION!
The NFF had an emergency meeting as a consequence of Coach Oliseh's unprecedented reaction. It was reported that at the meeting, some NFF members suggested the outright sacking of Coach Oliseh! But other NFF members including the NFF's chairman, prevailed on the disgruntled NFF members for Coach Oliseh to be given another chance.
This was done, and Coach Oliseh stayed on the job- albeit with benefit of hindsight- temporarily!
The author in an article on the " Nigerian World Forum" titled :" Coach Sunday Oliseh should please watch his steps, before it becomes too late!,"(https://nigeriaworld.com/feature/publication/nwokeji/022216.html) , cautioned Coach Oliseh on the need to thread softly in his dealings with the public.

"THE RATHER SURPRISING RESIGNATION OF COACH SUNDAY OLISEH"
The above title is the title of the article written by the author, on the "Nigeria World forum,"(https://nigeriaworld.com/feature/publication/nwokeji/030616.html), to exclaim the author's surprise at the unexpected resignation of Coach Oliseh, as coach of the Super Eagles of Nigeria!

It was indeed shocking news to Nigerians. The author had tried in his articles in the " Nigeria World Forum," to shore up Coach Oliseh, as a consequence of the myriad of criticisms he received as a result of Nigeria's early ouster from the "CHAN" competition. But all of the author's efforts were in vain, as Coach Oliseh, apparently, had made up his mind to quit the Super Eagles' job, as a consequence of the negative reactions that followed Nigeria's early ouster from the "CHAN" competition.
He cited poor working conditions occasioned by an uncooperative NFF, as reasons for his resignation.
The author in the above- mentioned article disagreed!

THE NFF'S REACTION TO COACH OLISEH'S RESIGNATION
The NFF's Chairman: Mr. Amaju Pinnick, in a speech in the United States of America, expressed his disappointment at the performance of Nigerian coaches of the Super Eagles. Mr. Pinnick it must be recalled, earlier on, tried in vain to persuade Coach Oliseh to stay on the job, when Coach Oliseh intimated him of his intentions to resign.
He regretted that Nigerian coaches couldn't effectively function as "managers" of the Super Eagles of Nigeria!
It was clear from his sentiments, where the NFF would go shopping for the next substantive coach of the Super Eagles.

POST MORTEM ANALYSIS: THE COACH SUNDAY OLISEH ERA!
Coach Sunday Oliseh got a job that was and still is the dream of many an ex-Nigerian soccer international, and that on a platter of gold for that matter; but unfortunately, and with all due respects, messed up the opportunity!
He was selected as coach of the Super Eagles, with virtually little or no previous coaching experience; and with no competition from anybody! These unusual advantages notwithstanding, he showed from the very first day on the job, that he wasn't equal to the task. In his very first press conference, he committed the blunder of saying that only players who plied their trade in the first division would be invited to the Super Eagles. He was later to go back on this assertion.
He also had difficulties managing the egos of certain Super Eagles' players. This reached a critical point with his altercation with Goalkeeper Vincent Enyeama, that resulted in the pre-mature retirement of the former Super Eagles' skipper. While the author does not heap all the blame for the problem with Goalkeeper Vincent Enyeama on Coach Oliseh, but the author believes that if Coach Oliseh had handled the matter with the needed maturity, the problem could have been resolved peacefully.
Coach Oliseh made another mistake by his appointment of Ahmed Musa, as substantive Super Eagles' skipper. By so doing he bypassed the already existing tradition of appointment of the oldest serving player as Super Eagles' skipper! Following this tradition, John Mikel Obi, should have been appointed skipper and not Ahmed Musa. The consequence of bypassing tradition in the appointment of Super Eagles' skipper cannot be overemphasized! Coach Samson Sia Sia, fortuitously, corrected this anomaly, by reversing Coach Oliseh's decision and, consequently, made John Obi Mikel, substantive skipper of the Super Eagles of Nigeria.

Coach Oliseh, apparently, had problems with his health. He once left the Super Eagles' camp pre-maturely on account of ill-health. This certainly didn't help matters.

Tactically, his organization of the team was questionable. The defense was the Achilles heel of the team. This mainly accounted for their pre-mature elimination from the CHAN competition!

Coach Oliseh also had difficulties coping with public criticisms of his performance as Super Eagles' coach. As Super Eagles' coach, and the man with the biggest coaching job in Africa, he was certainly the cynosure of many eyes and certainly open to public scrutiny and criticisms! The author advised him in the article titled:" Coach Sunday Oliseh should please watch his steps, before it becomes too late!," published on the "Nigeria World forum,"(https://nigeriaworld.com/feature/publication/nwokeji/022216.html), to hire the services of a public relations officer to help him in this regard.

Coach Oliseh, apparently, had little or no fighting spirit, as Super Eagles' coach; he gave up too easily, in the face of pressure; no Super Eagles' or any other soccer coach for that matter, succeeds without having a fighter's mentality/ fighting spirit!

Coach Oliseh, was apparently, a temperamental, arrogant, stubborn coach, with a low tolerance level for public criticisms! These characteristics certainly contributed to making him unqualified for the job of Super Eagles' coach; certainly at the time he was hired!

In conclusion, with benefit of hindsight, the appointment of Coach Oliseh, was one huge blunder committed by the NFF. The author, has nothing personally against Coach Oliseh; as a matter of fact, the author loves him as a person and admired him greatly as a player; but with regards his performance as Super Eagles' coach, with all due respects, he was a disaster!

Nigeria (the Super Eagles of Nigeria and Nigerians), paid a huge price for his seven months on the job! The author articulated these sentiments in the article titled :" The Rather Surprising Resignation of Coach Sunday Oliseh", on the "Nigeria World Forum,"(https://nigeriaworld.com/feature/publication/nwokeji/030616.html).

As a Super Eagles' player, he was excellent; as Super Eagles' coach, he was a disaster and has unfortunately earned for himself the reputation of : "Run-away" coach.

CHAPTER 6
THE BRIEF ERA OF COACH SAMSON SIA SIA +CONCLUSIONS

The unexpected resignation of Coach Sunday Oliseh, necessitated the appointment of Coach Samson Sia Sia, on an interim basis as coach of the Super Eagles of Nigeria.

The expectation for Coach Sia Sia was: qualification for the 2017 Nations' cup competition. Realistically, this expectation now appeared difficult to attain, more especially, considering the events of the period that followed the sacking of Coach Keshi. Nigeria's Super Eagles' fortunes had sunk to new lows even before the first ball was kicked against Egypt, Nigeria's then next opponents!

The above- mentioned facts notwithstanding, Coach Samson Sia Sia, was expected to perform, and he went about his task in all earnest.

Coach Samson Sia Sia, started by inviting a number of locally-based players to the Super Eagles camp, for an initial screening process.

After this phase of the preparatory process was completed, Coach Samson Sia Sia invited a number of foreign-based players, to complement the remaining locally-based players.

THE APPOINTMENT OF JOHN MIKEL OBI AS SUPER EAGLES' CAPTAIN!

While all the players were in camp, Coach Samson Sia Sia, at a press conference, announced the appointment of John Obi Mikel as the new Super Eagles' substantive captain.

He replaced the former Skipper, Ahmed Musa, who voluntarily relinquished his captaincy of the team, in favor of John Obi Mikel!

NIGERIA VERSUS EGYPT,25TH MARCH,2016, in KADUNA, NIGERIA.

The Super Eagles of Nigeria, took on the "Pharaohs" of Egypt, in a 2017 Nations' cup decider! It was a match that would determine the winner of the sole ticket in the group, for participation at the 2017 AFCON competition.

To motivate the Super Eagles, the author wrote an article titled: "Super Eagles of Nigeria: Remembering the 4-0 'demolition' of the Egyptians in 1977",(https://nigeriaworld.com/feature/publication/nwokeji/031716.html) , in the "Nigeria World forum"!

The "Ahmadu Bello" stadium, was jammed to capacity with the mammoth crowd that thronged the stadium on the day of the match.

Some of the spectators, even climbed to unconventional places around the stadium to watch the match! This unconventional behavior of some spectators, earned Nigeria a fine from the "Confederation of African Football- CAF"!

It was a match the Super Eagles had to win and get at least a draw in the return leg, in Egypt, to stand a good chance of qualification for the 2017 AFCON competition.

Coach Samson Sia Sia, made no pretensions of his intention to get at least the desired result against Egypt; he even talked of winning both legs against Egypt!

Super Eagles' players like: Skipper John Obi Mikel and Victor Obinna Nsofor, were in agreement with their coach.

On match day, the following players lined-up for Nigeria:

Goalkeeper Carl Ikeme, was in goal. The defense line consisted of: Abdullahi Shehu, at right back; Stanley Amuzie, left back; Efe Ambrose, centre-half back and Godfrey Oboabona, left-half back.

The mid-field consisted of: Etebo Oghenekaro, defensive mid-field; Skipper John Obi Mikel, central mid-field; Simon Moses, left-sided offensive mid-fielder and Ahmed Musa, right-sided offensive.
The offensive front had: Odion Ighalo, as deepest striker and Kelechi Iheanacho, as supporting striker.
The Super Eagles played in a 4-4-2 formation.
The Super Eagles kicked off and dominated the game. They pressurized the Egyptians and came close to scoring on a number of occasions, but were constantly thwarted by the solid Egyptian defense and their good goalkeeper. The Super Eagles kept on coming, but could not score. The Egyptians always tried to counter- attack, and nearly scored one occasion, but for the intervention of Goalkeeper Carl Ikeme.
The Super Eagles dominance in the first half, was reflected in the superior ball possession: Nigeria 67% ; Egypt 23%.
The Super Eagles' superior ball possession didn't result in goals, and the first half ended, scoreless.
In the second half, the same pattern continued, this time around with some measure of success for the Super Eagles of Nigeria. They scored in the 60th minute, through Etebo Oghenekaro, who connected from a rebound, off a lob by Kelechi Iheanacho, which beat the Egyptian goalkeeper, but hit the upright of the Egyptian goal post, for Nigeria's first goal!
Nigerians cheered wildly!
 However, their joy was rudely interrupted when in the 90th minute, the Egyptians took advantage of a lapse in concentration of the Nigerians to score the equalizer, by Ahmed Salah!
The match, ended, 1-1, both sides shared the points, one a piece!

POST MATCH PRESS CONFERENCE
Nigerians were disappointed they gave up two points at the last minute to Egypt, as a consequence of the drawn match, which made both teams share one point each, instead of the three points that would have accrued the Super Eagles, in the event of a win.
The Nigerian journalists who were disappointed, queried Coach Sia Sia's tactical choices, by giving up a quasi certain victory at the last minute!
Coach Sia Sia, answered that he thought a loss of concentration on the part of the Super Eagles' defenders caused the Egyptian equalizer.
He like Skipper John Obi Mikel, thought beating the Egyptians at home, in the return leg was realizable!

NIGERIA VERSUS EGYPT, 29TH MARCH, 2016, IN ALEXANDRIA, EGYPT.
In the return leg, in Egypt, the Super Eagles went to the encounter, with the mindset to win!
Coach Sia Sia, made some changes to the team that played in Kaduna:
He replaced Goalkeeper Carl Ikeme, who couldn't travel as a consequence of some health issues, with Goalkeeper Daniel Akpeyi.
He brought in Victor Moses into the mid-field to take the place of Oghenekaro Etebo; who was moved to the left-sided offensive mid-field position.

He dropped Moses Simon and Kelechi Iheanacho. He introduced Aminu Umar as striking partner to Odion Ighalo.

The Super Eagles played in a 4-4-2 formation.

Like in the first leg match, they dominated proceedings, but could not score. The Egyptians exhibited to near perfection their compact defensive formation.

The first half, ended, scoreless.

In the second half, the Egyptians came more into the picture, and nearly scored but for the timely intervention of Nigeria's goalkeeper.

However, mother luck smiled on them, in the 65th minute, when a badly cleared corner –kick, taken by the Egyptians resulted in a goal mouth scramble ; the Egyptians took advantage to score the lone goal of the match, which proved to be the winner!

The Super Eagles reacted forcefully, by pressurizing the Egyptians but to no avail. A goal-bound shot fired from about thirty meters from the Egyptian goal area, by Nigeria's Victor Moses, beat the Egyptian goalkeeper, but hit the Egyptian goal post and was kicked away by the Egyptian defenders! It was a close sheave that might have given the Super Eagles the equalizer!

The Super Eagles lost the match, 1-0; and, thus, failed to qualify for AFCON 2017; for the second consecutive time!

Their last group's match against Tanzania, was for the statistics.

THE DAY AFTER THE FAILED QUALIFICATION FOR AFCON 2017

Nigerians were devastated at yet another AFCON failure!

The technical crew sensing the mood of the nation, wrote an apology letter to Nigerians; but noted that the team was already 'broken' when they took over management of the team, about a month to the encounter with the Egyptians! The author is in full agreement.

Nigerians were so enraged that some soccer commentators called for the resignation of the NFF chairman: Mr. Amaju Pinnick!; for what they called his administrative incompetence, that led to failure to qualify for AFCONS:2015 and 2017!

POST-MORTEM ANALYSIS: THE COACH SAMSON SIA SIA ERA!

Coach Samson Sia Sia, cannot be honestly evaluated based on two matches.

Coach Sia Sia, was contracted to coach a team in crisis! It was clear the damage had been done before he came on board.

The combined consequences of the failures in soccer administration, in the immediate aftermath of the 2014 World cup competition in Brazil and in the immediate aftermath of the failure for qualification for AFCON 2015, resulted in the failure for qualification for AFCON 2017!

The author in an article on the "Nigerian world forum" titled "AFCON 2017: Another failure for the Super Eagles of Nigeria,"

(https://nigeriaworld.com/feature/publication/nwokeji/041016.html), articulated the reasons for Nigeria's failure to qualify for AFCON 2017.

Coach Samson Sia Sia , with benefit of hindsight, should be congratulated for agreeing to coach the Super Eagles at a time the team was in deep trouble, occasioned by the aforementioned problems.

CHAPTER 7
THE BRIEF ERA OF COACH SALISU YUSUF

While the NFF, sought to redefine itself, vis-vis the next substantive coach of the Super Eagles, in the immediate aftermath of the failure to qualify for AFCON 2017, the hour of the next international engagements for the Super Eagles came.
The NFF decided to go for an interim coaching arrangement, as a stop gap measure pending the appointment of a substantive foreign coach. This interim coach was to oversee the next matches of the Super Eagles of Nigeria.
The author who was not impressed with the pro-active steps taken by the NFF, in the immediate aftermath of the elimination for AFCON 2017, and not wanting another failure for the Super Eagles, wrote the following articles in the "Nigeria World forum", to further remind the NFF of the urgency of the situation: " NFF: Please, no more tardiness in the appointment of a substantive Super Eagles' coach;"
(https://nigeriaworld.com/feature/publication/nwokeji/0410016.html), and " NFF: The interim coaches' arrangement for the Super Eagles of Nigeria is a certain recipe for another failure!,"
(https://nigeriaworld.com/feature/publication/nwokeji/042516.html).

NIGERIA VERSUS MALI, 27th May, 2016.
The Super Eagles of Nigeria, took on the Malian national team, in France, in an international friendly match, on the aforementioned date.
The Super Eagles were under the coaching guidance of Coach Salisu Yusuf; who functioned as interim coach.
The Super Eagles won the friendly encounter, 1-0; courtesy of a goal scored by Kelechi Iheanacho, in the 77th minute.

NIGERIA VERSUS LUXEMBOURG, 31st May, 2016.
The Super Eagles of Nigeria, next played the national team of Luxembourg in an international friendly, in Luxembourg city, Luxembourg.
The Super Eagles easily won the encounter, 3-1; courtesy of goals by:
Brown Ideye, in the 36th minute; Kelechi Iheanacho, in the 69th minute and Odion Ighalo, in the 93rd minute.

THE AFTERMATH OF THE FRIENDLIES
In the aftermath of the friendlies won under the guidance of Coach Salisu Yusuf, some Super Eagles' players, starting campaigning for the retention of Coach Yusuf, as substantive Super Eagles' coach.
They claimed he had a good relationship with the players and was tactically sound enough to coach the Super Eagles of Nigeria.

The author, disagreed, because of the enormity of the task ahead: the crucial 2018 World cup qualifiers; where the Super Eagles were grouped in a group of death!

CONCLUSIONS ON THE BRIEF ERA OF COACH SALISU YUSUF
Coach Salisu Yusuf was in charge for too short a period of time to be assessed. Thus, a post-mortem analysis cannot be done.

CHAPTER 8
THE ERA OF COACH GERNOT ROHR

The appointment of a foreign coach for the Super Eagles of Nigeria, was difficult to achieve. Nigerians were very much divided with regards who would be the substantive coach of the Super Eagles.
Some Nigerian soccer 'nationalists' felt the country had advanced so much in soccer that the employment of a foreign tactician was tantamount to insulting the country's status in soccer!
Other Nigerians, to whose group the author belonged, believed the country needed a foreign coach, in view of the enormity of the task ahead in the 2018 World cup qualification series! The author felt Nigeria needed a foreign coach, who would not only be tactically and technically sound, but would be unbiased in the selection of players and most importantly, would be above aboard in the discharge of his duties- a coach who would rise above the vices which bedevil some Nigerian coaches, and prevent them from discharging their responsibilities adequately!
Considering the need not to fail again, Nigeria needed to be represented at the 2018 World cup competition!
The NFF, towed the line of thinking of the group of Nigerians to which the author belonged.
The Federal government made it absolutely clear to the NFF, it didn't have the financial capability to employ a foreign tactician!
The NFF under the leadership of: Mr. Amaju Pinnick, was resolute in its determination to have a foreign coach in place for the Super Eagles of Nigeria!
The NFF, thus, sourced the financing of the Super Eagles' coach's salary elsewhere. Luckily for Nigeria, a unnamed private business organization, accepted to take up sponsorship of the Super Eagles' coach's salary.
When the hurdle of the Super Eagles' coach's salary was crossed, the NFF intensified its search for a foreign coach.
The search light fell on an unnamed French coach, whom yours sincerely suspected was Coach Paul Le Guen. Coach Le Guen, like most foreign coaches, was and apparently, still is a great admirer of the Super Eagles of Nigeria.

To this club of foreign coaches, who admired and still admire the Super Eagles of Nigeria are: Coaches: Carlo Ancelloti; Sven Goran Eriksson; Berti Voghts; Clemence Westerhoff; Bonfre Jo; Ruud Gullit; Alejandro Sabella; Claude Le roy; Arigo Sacchi; Glen Hoddle; Goran Stepanovic; Rene Havre , who is the current Moroccan coach, who when it was speculated shortly before the 2010 World cup competition, that he was being considered for the Super Eagles' coaching job, said if Nigeria wanted him, he was ready to trek on foot from Angola(the venue of the 2010 AFCON which was then just concluded, and where he coached Zambia, to the quarter-finals), to Nigeria, to sign the dotted lines to be the Super Eagles' substantive coach!

The negotiations with Coach Paul Le Guen, went well, and he looked set to be the new Super Eagles' substantive coach. He had even talked of how the job of Super Eagles coach, was a dream job to him. And how he had already started a compilation of the list of Super Eagles' players!

It was at a point in time, reported in the press, that he was going to be the next Super Eagles coach.

However, before he could sign the dotted lines, he disagreed with the NFF, over his place of abode! While he wanted to maintain his place of residence in France, and to be jetting in and out of Nigeria, in the discharge of his duties; the NFF, preferred a coach who would live in Nigeria. Also, he disagreed with the clause that his contract continuing or not, would depend on Nigeria's qualification of the 2018 World cup tournament.

As a consequence, the temporary arrangement with Coach Le Guen, fell into the water!

The NFF, thus, had to extend its search; this time to Germany. The negotiations with Coach Gernot Rohr, went smoothly. As a consequence, Coach Rohr, had to abandon the soccer development programme, he was supervising for the German football Association, to coach the Super Eagles of Nigeria.

He was initially, contracted by the NFF, for a two-year period. One of the clauses in his contract, which he signed at a rather subdued ceremony at an Abuja hotel, was - the qualification of Nigeria for the 2018 World cup competition!

Coach Rohr, right from the onset, not only believed in the qualification, but believed the Super Eagles of Nigeria, would get to the later stages of the 2018 World cup competition!

With that uncanny self-assurance, Coach Rohr, went to work in earnest. The author must point out that the signing ceremony for Coach Rohr's contract, was subdued, apparently, because of the then non-reception of a foreign Super Eagles' coach, by a cross section of Nigerians! The salary of the coach, apparently, for a similar reason was and is still being kept secret. As earlier mentioned, the identity of the sponsors of Coach Rohr's salary, is still being kept secret!

Coach Rohr, thus, stealthily started work as Super Eagles' coach, knowing fully well, the only way to convince Nigerians is through producing good results for the Super Eagles of Nigeria!

When Coach Rohr took over as Super Eagles' coach, he made an analysis of the team, and came to the conclusion that the team lacked a solid defense. Coach Rohr's thinking was that if the Super Eagles defended well, they would concede less goals, and if they conceded less goals, they would win more matches!

Thus, he set about looking for capable defenders, who would do his bidding.

He already had two solid central defenders in : William Troost Ekong, alias "Rock of Gibralter" and "Commander-General" Leon Balogun.

He set about looking for other defenders. The full- back spots, were problematic. At left back, was the "Recalcitrant" Elderson Echiejile, whose form was not constant. But somehow still became Coach Rohr's first choice left back, for the period of the 2018 World cup qualification matches.

The search for the other defenders was ongoing when the hour of the next international match came calling.

NIGERIA VERSUS TANZANIA, ON 3rd SEPTEMBER, 2016, IN UYO, NIGERIA.

The Super Eagles of Nigeria, took on the "Taifa Stars" of Tanzania, in the "Goodswil Akpabio International Stadium," Uyo. The match was the last match of the qualification series for the "AFCON 2017."

The match was a "dead rubber" encounter, since both teams had already been eliminated for the "AFCON 2017" competition.

The following Super Eagles players lined out for Nigeria:

Goalkeeper Carl Ikeme, was in goal. The Defenders were: Musa Muhammed(who was being tried as right back), right back; "The Recalcitrant" Elderson Echiejile, left-back; William Troost Ekong, centre-half back and Leon Balogun, left-half back.

The mid-fielders were: Ogenyi Onazi, alias the "angry wasp who chases his opponents to hell", defensive mid-fielder; The tactically erudite Skipper John Obi Mikel, central mid-field.

The attackers were: The "Supersonic Jet-heeled" Ahmed "Mansa" Musa, right winger; The "Silvery, silky, flowery-skilled, ubiquitous and magnificent" Victor Moses, left winger; Odion Ighalo, alias "Top 9", centre-forward and The "Predaciously predacious" Kelechi Iheanacho, supporting striker.

The Super Eagles in their 4-2-4 formation, dominated the game from the beginning to the end; but found scoring difficult. The very brilliant Tanzanian goalkeeper, stood between Nigeria and goal!

Finally, a fine lobbed shot by Kelechi Iheanacho, in the 79th minute, made the difference, as the Super Eagles defeated the "Taifa Stars" of Tanzania,1-0.

The three points were collected by the Super Eagles; but it was a result for the statistics books!

REFLECTIONS ON COACH ROHR'S FIRST MATCH

Coach Rohr impressed the author, in his very first match in charge of the Super Eagles. He organized a friendly match with a local team – "Akwa United," before the encounter with the Tanzanians. Thus, in a space of four days that the Super Eagles were in camp for the Tanzanian match, they played two matches, and during this short period of camping, he saw all the invited players in action! This certainly helped him in assessing all the invited players; and by implication, in the building of the Super Eagles team.

NIGERIA VERSUS ZAMBIA, 9th OCTOBER, 2016, IN NDOLA, ZAMBIA.
The Super Eagles of Nigeria, were grouped in the so called "group of death," for the 2018 World cup qualifiers. They were grouped together with: Cameroun, Algeria and Zambia.
Only the group's winner qualified for the 2018 World cup competition.
All the teams in the Super Eagles World cup group have been African champions, at least on one occasion! Cameroun, was the then reigning African champions.
This was the reason the group was called the "group of death"!
The Super Eagles' coach: Gernot Rohr, knowing the enormity of the task ahead of the Super Eagles, went into the Zambian match, with the mindset of victory, over the Zambians, even in their backyard!
On match day, the following players filled out for Nigeria:
Goalkeeper Carl Ikeme, was in goal. The defenders were: Wilfred Ndidi, right back(this was another experimentation of Coach Rohr's, at right back); Elderson Echiejile, left-back; William Troost-Ekong, centre-half back; "Field Marshal" Kenneth Omeruo, left-half back.
The mid-fielders were: Ogenyi Onazi, defensive mid-field; Skipper John Mikel Obi, central mid-field; Simon Moses, alias the "Atilogwu dancer," right-sided wing offensive mid-fielder and Alex Iwobi, alias the "dancing Krekel," left-sided wing offensive mid-fielder.
The attackers were: Kelechi Iheanacho, deepest striker and Brown Ideye, supporting striker.
The Super Eagles played in a: 4-4-2 formation.
The Super Eagles took over control of the game from the onset and attacked the Zambians. This resulted in clear opportunities, which were utilized by the Super Eagles to score two goals: Alex Iwobi, in the 32nd minute; and Kelechi Iheanacho, in the 42th minute!
The Super Eagles led 2-0, at half time.
The author who watched the match, was happy at the Super Eagles' lead ; and told my Brazilian neighbor what was happening and hoped for a good result at the end of the day.
It was indeed hoping for all Super Eagles' supporters, as the Zambians, who appeared out-matched and out-played in the first half, now 'resurrected' in the second half, and controlled the game, and pushed the Super Eagles back into their own territory.
The Super Eagles supporters were at the edge of their seats as the highly brilliant Zambians scored a goal in the 71st minute, to reduce the tally, to 2-1.

The Zambian onslaught continued; at this juncture, Coach Rohr, had to call in his technical expertise, in order to safe guard the three points, that appeared to be going the way of Nigeria.

He replaced striker Brown Ideye, with defensive mid-fielder, Anderson Esiti, and changed the formation from: 4-4-2, to 4-5-1, a more defensive/mid-field-oriented formation, in other to contain the rampaging Zambians. This was successful; the replacement of Ogenyi Onazi, with Shehu Abdullahi, alias "Man-O- War", was meant to further strengthen the defensive mid-field position, and make life more difficult for the Zambians. The replacement of Simon Moses with Ahmed Musa, was meant to threaten the Zambians in an offensive disposition. And that way further take away their threat to the Super Eagles.

These changes were all successful and the Super Eagles won the match,2-1, and came home, with all three points at stake, to take the lead in their group!

THE DAY AFTER THE MATCH AGAINST THE ZAMBIANS

The Zambians took the result of the match like true sports men and women. The Zambians were reported to have lined up after the match to get the autographs of certain Super Eagles' players; more especially, John Obi Mikel!

The Federal Government congratulated the Super Eagles, and wished them more grease to their elbows.

NIGERIA VERSUS ALGERIA, 12TH NOVEMBER, 2016, IN UYO, NIGERIA.

In the build –up to the Algerian match, the Nigerian first choice goalkeeper: Carl Ikeme, was injured and couldn't play for Nigeria. Nigeria had to use the second choice goalkeeper. Considering Carl Ikeme's stature as a goalkeeper, and the relatively unknown replacement, and also considering the reputation of the Algerians, Nigerians were somewhat apprehensive about the outcome of the match; more especially, from the goalkeeping point of view!

The Algerians had a great reputation as a good soccer nation; but the Algerian team of the 2018 World cup qualifiers, appeared somewhat weaker than the Algerian teams of the '80s and '90s.

These facts about the Algerian team notwithstanding, Nigerians were still somewhat apprehensive about the possible outcome of the match.

Skipper John Mikel Obi, as a mark of respect for the Algerians, said a drawn result against the Algerians, was also a good result.

It was reported that a particular Nigerian player, reported late to camp, and with a very expensive car; this player had been in town earlier on, but reported late to camp. Coach Rohr, apparently, in anger, decided to make him start the match from the substitute's bench, as punitive measure!

The Algerians on their part, also had a measure of drama; their Serbian coach, who coached them in their opening group's match against Cameroun, was sacked shortly afterwards, as a result of players' 'mutiny'!

The following players started the match for Nigeria:

Goalkeeper Daniel Akpeyi, was in goal.

The defence featured:

Kenneth Omeruo, right- back; Elderson Echiejile, left-back. William Troost-Ekong, centre-half back; and Leon Balogun, left-half back.
The mid-field had the following players:
Ogenyi Onazi, defensive mid-field; Etebo Oghenekaro, alias "Turbo Engine", defensive mid-field; Skipper John Obi Mikel, offensive/central mid-field. Victor Moses, right-sided offensive mid-fielder; Alex Iwobi, left-sided offensive mid-fielder.
Kelechi Iheanacho, was the lone central striker.

The Super Eagles played in a 4-2-3-1 formation.
The match kicked off and the Super Eagles wanting a win, went after the Algerians. Victor Moses, missed a goal- scoring opportunity, in the second minute of the game. However, he made up for the miss, by scoring in the 25th minute of play!
John Mikel Obi, scored the second goal in the forty-first minute, to bring scores to 2-0, at half time.
In the second half, the Algerians woke up from their slumber, and took control of the game. The Super Eagles, were left chasing shadows. Like in the game against the Zambians, they appeared to have lost steam, in the second half!
The Algerians took advantage of the situation to score a beautiful goal, fired home from about thirty meters to Nigeria's goal area! The Algerians, in their resurgence, missed a number of opportunities, that might have made life more difficult for the Super Eagles of Nigeria.
Coach Rohr, like in the Zambian match, weighed in technically and tactically, by bringing in Ahmed Musa, to replace Alex Iwobi; this was meant to shore up the offensive line of Nigeria, and put the Algerians under more pressure, and that way reduce their forays into the Nigerian area. The substitution, fell in line with the popular soccer maxim: that the best way to defend is to attack!
Coach Rohr, also introduced Wilfred Ndidi, in the place of Skipper John Mikel Obi, to shore up the offensive mid-field; and that way put more pressure on the Algerians.
The injured Kenneth Omeruo, was replaced by Abdullahi Shehu.
These changes were successful for the Super Eagles, as they scored a third goal in the 92nd minute; off a beautiful wing offensive play by Ahmed Musa, which resulted in Victor Moses, finishing off a beautiful pull-out by Ahmed Musa, to bring the final result at:3-1, in Nigeria's favour!
The Super Eagles, thus, collected all three points at stake, to take a firm lead in their group; and make Nigerians to start dreaming of another World cup participation, in 2018!

THE DAY AFTER THE MATCH
Nigerians were happy at another positive ending to a World cup qualification campaign! They gradually started believing in yet another World cup qualification.
A friend of the author's, confidently told the author, Nigeria had the players to get the 2018 World cup ticket!

Other Nigerians expressed worries about what they considered the Super Eagles' mid-field frailties, occasioned by the near collapse of the Super Eagles' mid-field, in the second half!
The Federal Government once again congratulated the Super Eagles of Nigeria.
The author, in an article on the "Nigeria World forum," recognised the latest successes of the Super Eagles of Nigeria, while of course expressing concerns about the Super Eagles' mid-field, with an article titled: "A Super Eagles' Renaissance?"
(https://nigeriaworld.com/feature/publication/nwokeji/111916.html)

NIGERIA VERSUS SENEGAL, 23rd MARCH, 2017, IN BARNET, ENGALND.
The Super Eagles of Nigeria, gathered in Barnet, England, for preparations for two friendly matches: against Senegal and – Burkina-Faso.
The gathering of the Super Eagles, in England, served as an opportunity, to try out new players invited to the team, for example: Isaac Success Ajayi; Noel Bazee; Olanrewaju Kayode; and also to try to convince players like: Tyronne "The Dream" Ebuehi; and Ola Aina, to play for Nigeria.
The players who had not yet decided to play for Nigeria, but who were in England with the rest of the Nigerian team, were given the chance to be with the rest of the Super Eagles players in camp, train with them, and generally see the way things were done in the Super Eagles' camp, with a view to helping them make up their minds with regards their international allegiance.
With benefit of hindsight, the camping in England, helped swing the pendulum, in Nigeria's favour, as Tyronne Ebuehi and Ola Aina, later on, decided to commit their international soccer future to Nigeria!
The Super Eagles of Nigeria, took on the Senegalese "Lions", on the aforementioned date, at the "Hive stadium."
The Super Eagles – though not at full strength- put up an inspired performance against the Senegalese, that played with the full complement of their national team.
The Senegalese scored in the 54th minute, as a consequence of a poorly treated corner-kick by Goalkeeper Daniel Akpeyi.
The Super Eagles fought back and got the deserved equaliser, in the 83rd minute, through a resultant penalty kick, taken by Kelechi Iheanacho, after he was brought down in the Senegalese penalty box.
The match, ended, 1-1.

NIGERIA VERSUS BURKINA-FASO, 27TH MARCH, 2017.
The match against Burkina-Faso, on the aforementioned date at the "Hive Stadium," couldn't take place because the Burkinabe team couldn't get entry visas to the UK. This was certainly to the consternation of the Nigerians.
Coach Gernot Rohr, not wanting to waste the scheduled date for the match, decided to play a "practice match", with the Super Eagles team. In other words, all the Super Eagles players were grouped in two teams that played each other in a practice match.

The players who at that time had not made up their minds to play for Nigeria, took part in the practice match.

NIGERIA VERSUS CORSICA, 26TH MAY, 2017.
The Super Eagles of Nigeria as part of preparations for their 2019 Nations' cup qualifier against South-Africa, took on the National team of Corsica, in a friendly encounter, in France.
The Super Eagles team that was not at full strength, took on the Corsicans, at their home, and met a difficult opponent.
The Corsicans took the lead early in the game, through a penalty kick awarded them in the 2nd minute of play.
The Nigerians rallied back, out-played the Corsicans, created a myriad of chances, but could not take them, as a consequence of a very good Corsican goalkeeper!
This Corsican goalkeeper, stood between the Super Eagles and the goals!
The Super Eagles were however lucky to escape defeat as Kelechi Iheanacho, converted an 81st minute penalty, to equalise and end the game, at 1-1.

NIGERIA VERSUS TOGO, 1ST JUNE, 2017.
The Super Eagles of Nigeria, took on the Togolese national team, the "Hawks", in Paris, France, in a second friendly match, geared towards preparing the Super Eagles for the encounter against the South-Africans, in a 2019 AFCON qualifier.
The Super Eagles scored three first half goals in the : 2nd, 18th and 28th minutes, by Ahmed Musa, who scored the first two goals and Kelechi Iheanacho, who scored the third and last goal.
The Super Eagles won the match, 3-0!

NIGERIA VERSUS SOUTH-AFRICA, 10th JUNE, 2017, UYO, NIGERIA.
The Super Eagles of Nigeria, for the preparatory phase of the encounter with South-Africa, played two friendly matches in France, as earlier mentioned. Coach Gernot Rohr, used the opportunity, to try out a number of younger players.
Apparently, because of the quality of the opposition, he decided to give quite a number of the younger players a chance, in the match against South-Africa. In other words, in the match against South-Africa, Coach Rohr, used essentially an under-23 side! This was one decision he later regretted.
In the match against South-Africa, the following players lined out for Nigeria:
Goalkeeper Daniel Akpeyi, was in goal. He replaced the first choice keeper: Carl Ikeme, who was injured.
The back four were: Abdullahi Shehu, right-back; Elderson Echiejile, left-back; William Troost- Ekong, centre-half back and Chidozie Awaziem, left-half back.

The mid-fielders were: Stand-in Skipper Ogenyi Onazi, defensive mid-fielder; Wilfred Ndidi, central mid-fielder; Etebo Ogenekaro, box-to-box mid-fielder.
The attackers were: Simon Moses, winger; Alex Iwobi, winger and Kelechi Iheanacho, centre-forward.
The Super Eagles played in a 4-3-3 formation.
They went into the offensive from the blast of the whistle. And probed deeply into the South-African vital area, but the chances that came about, were wasted. This scenario, continued for a greater part of the first half.
However, towards the end of the first half, the South-Africans came more into the picture; and began threatening the Nigerians. They came quite close to scoring on a number of occasions!
The first half, ended, scoreless.
In the second half, the South-Africans further upped their game, and came closer to the Super Eagles vital area on a number of occasions. During one of those occasions, in the 53th minute, they scored a goal, through their central striker, off a glancing header, off a pull-out from a South-African winger!
With scores at Nigeria 0, South-Africa1, the Super Eagles further upped their game. Coach Rohr, made some changes, but these were not effective; as the South –Africans, scored a second goal, in the 80th minute, through a counter-attack that slide open the entire Nigerian defence; and left the Nigerian goalkeeper helpless, in the face of the onrushing South-African attacker.
A nervous Coach Rohr could be seen pacing up and down the coaches' territory, shouting frantic instructions at the Super Eagles' players. But to no avail!
South-Africa, defeated Nigeria, for the first time, and on home soil for that matter: 2-0!

THE DAY AFTER THE DEFEAT TO THE SOUTH-AFRICANS
Nigerians were in shock at what happened! Some Nigerian commentators heaped all the blame for the defeat on Goalkeeper Daniel Akpeyi!
The author didn't fully agree with them. The author chronicled his thoughts on what happened on that day, in an article on the "Nigeria World Forum," titled : "Lessons from the rather surprising and shocking defeat to the South-Africans."(https://nigeriaworld.com/feature/publication/nwokeji/062417.html)
Coach Rohr, was to regret his decision to have fielded an under-23 team against South-Africa! He described that defeat as the worst decision he made as coach of the Super Eagles!
Nigerians, however, 'forgave' him; but demanded from him victory in the match against the Camerounians, in the World cup qualifier; when they sighted Coach Rohr, at "Balogun Market" in Lagos!

NIGERIA VERSUS CAMEROUN, 1ST SEPTEMBER, 2017, UYO, NIGERIA.

In the preview to the double- header against the Camerounians, the author in an article titled: " Our expectations of the Super Eagles of Nigeria, in the double cracker against the Indomitable Lions of Cameroun!," on the "Nigeria World forum," (https://nigeriaworld.com/feature/publication/nwokeji/081517.html), gave his considered opinion on how the Super Eagles should thoroughly prepare for the Camerounians.

The Super Eagles took on the Camerounians, in a double-header match(two consecutive matches), in the 2018 World cup qualifying series!

The first leg took place at Uyo, Nigeria, on the above- mentioned date.

In the author's review of the encounter against South-Africa, the author among other things advised Coach Rohr to use more experienced players for the Super Eagles henceforth. Coach Rohr, listened, as the invited players against Cameroun were mainly experienced players.

This list included, Skipper John Obi Mikel and Victor Moses, who both missed the match against South-Africa.

However, there was a bombshell which shook the Super Eagles camp. First choice goalkeeper, Carl Ikeme, was diagnosed with Leukemia, during a routine pre-season medical examination, with his English club side: Wolverhampton Wanderers! Nigerians prayed for his recovery, and hoped he would recover quickly enough to be part of the Super Eagles' World cup party. With benefit of hindsight, Carl Ikeme, though recovered from Leukemie, never played for the Super Eagles again; his match against the Zambians, was his last match for Nigeria! After the course of treatment, he retired from soccer! He won thus, 10 caps for Nigeria!

One contentious issue, was the replacement for goalkeeper Daniel Akpeyi. As a consequence of what Nigerians generally considered his poor performance against South-Africa, it was imperative on the coaching crew that a replacement was needed in the game against Cameroun!

That lot fell on goalkeeper: Ikechukwu Ezenwa; Coach Rohr, promised Nigerians that goalkeeper Ezenwa, would be adequately covered up in the game against the Camerounians.

The following players started the match against Cameroun:

Goalkeeper Ikechukwu Ezenwa, was in goal.

Defenders:

Abdullahi Shehu, right back(he convinced Coach Rohr, through his performances, he was the best at right back); Elderson Echiejile, left back; William Troost-Ekong, centre-half back; Leon Balogun, left-half back.

Mid-fielders:

Ogenyi Onazi, defensive mid-fielder; Wilfred Ndidi, defensive mid-fielder; Skipper John Obi Mikel, offensive mid-fielder.

Attackers:

Victor Moses, winger; Simon Moses, winger and Odion Ighalo, centre-forward.

The Super Eagles played in a 4-3-3 formation.

They initially lost control of the game to the Camerounians, after kickoff, as the Camerounians dictated the pace of the game.

However, in the 28th minute, a beautiful pass from Skipper John Mikel Obi to Odion Ighalo, resulted in Odion Ighalo, outwitting a Camerounian defender, to score Nigeria's first goal!

Nigeria's second goal was scored by Skipper John Obi Mikel, off a corner kick taken by Victor Moses.
The Super Eagles led by 2-0, at half time.
In the second half, the onslaught on the Camerounians continued, as Nigeria scored two more goals from Victor Moses and Kelechi Iheanacho, in the 54th and 75th minutes, to give the Super Eagles an overwhelming 4-0 victory, over the Camerounians, and to inch their way closer to the World cup ticket, as a consequence of an additional three points in the kitty!

THE DAY AFTER THE MARVELOUS VICTORY OVER THE CAMEROUNIANS
Nigerians were super excited at this victory! A Nigerian friend of the author's told the author, he had not seen the sort of fantastic display put up by the Super Eagles against Cameroun, in a very long while! The author, was in agreement.
The author, appreciated the Super Eagles' performance against Cameroun, with the article titled : "A solid performance by the "Marvellous" Super Eagles of Nigeria!," on the "Nigeria World Forum,"
(https://nigeriaworld.com/feature/publication/nwokeji/091217.html).

NIGERIA VERSUS CAMEROUN, 4TH SEPTEMBER, 2017, IN YAOUNDE CAMEROUN.
The return leg took place in Yaounde, Cameroun. The Super Eagles with a few days rest after the encounter in Uyo, travelled to Cameroun for the return leg.
The confidence level was high among the Super Eagles' players, the coaching crew, officials and Nigerians generally!
A Nigerian friend of the author's told the author, he expected the Super Eagles to get at worst a drawn result in Cameroun.
The Super Eagles coaching crew, lined-up exactly the same team that started the match, in Uyo, Nigeria.
They faced a highly 'refurbished' Camerounian team that was determined to do battle with Super Eagles at home.
The Super Eagles started the match, playing with confidence. They met an equally determined hosts ready to put up a fight against the Super Eagles at home.
However, there was no stopping the Super Eagles going ahead in the 30th minute, through a beautiful shot taken by Simon Moses, from the edge of the Camerounian penalty box!
The Super Eagles led 1-0, at half time.
In the second half, the Camerounians, not wanting to lose at home for the first time since 1972, upped their game and put the Super Eagles under more pressure.
This resulted in a 75th minute equaliser, when the Nigerian goalkeeper, inadvertently brought down a Camerounian attacker, in trying to save a goal- ward Camerounian thrust; the resultant penalty was well utilised by Cameroun to level the scores at one a piece!
The game ended 1-1. And both sides shared one point each.
Cameroun, thus, avoided a home defeat!

THE DAY AFTER THE MATCH
Nigerians were happy the World cup ticket was in the horizon! The Super
Eagles needed a draw to get it in the next match against the "Chipolopolo"
of Zambia.

NIGERIA VERSUS ZAMBIA, 7TH OCTOBER, 2017.
The Super Eagles of Nigeria, needed a draw in the match-up with Zambia,
to be sure of qualification for the 2018 World cup finals.
Given the antecedents of Zambian teams with regards the Super Eagles of
Nigeria, the author wrote an article in the "Nigeria World Forum," titled "
Super Eagles of Nigeria: Please, no complacency against the unpredictable
"Chipolopolo" of
Zambia,"(https://nigeriaworld.com/feature/publication/nwokeji/092617.ht
ml), in which he cautioned the Super Eagles about the potential danger
posed by a Zambian team!
The Zambian team that played the Super Eagles in 2017, was a far cry
from the Zambian team that confronted the Super Eagles at home in 2016.
The team had been re-enforced with players from the under-20 team, that
took part in the 2017 under-20 World cup competition. It was thus a well
'refurbished' Zambian team, that met the Super Eagles in 2017!
The Super Eagles' coach, knowing these latest facts about the Zambians,
was understandably angry with a Super Eagles player who told the coach
before returning home to prepare to face the Zambians, that the match
against the Zambians was as good as won, even before the ball was
kicked! An understandably angry Coach Rohr, told him straight in the face
that if he had that mind set about the Zambian team, he didn't need to
return home for the match! Coach Rohr told the player he needed players
who would not take the Zambians for granted. With benefit of hindsight,
he was correct in his assessment of the Zambians!
On match day, a jam packed "Goodswil Akpabio International Stadium,"
was the theatre of battle between two teams trying to achieve their
'destinies' with regards the 2018 World cup competition.
The same Super Eagles players that started the match against Cameroun,
started against Zambia- "you don't change a winning team!"
The Zambians showed from the very first minute that they were no
"makkies," as they matched the Super Eagles, 'grit-for- grit.' It was clear
the Super Eagles were in for a battle!
There was virtually no headway into the Zambian vital area, for the Super
Eagles, notwithstanding the superior ball possession of the Super Eagles of
Nigeria.
The Zambians even threatened the Super Eagles occasionally, through
dangerous counters!
The first half, ended, scoreless.
In the second half, the Zambians continued being difficult to deal with.
At this juncture, Coach Rohr, wanting to win the game for Nigeria, decided
to make what turned out to be a : "golden change for Nigeria!"
He brought in Alex Iwobi, to replace Moses Simon.

Before the match, Coach Rohr said he couldn't make up his mind whom to start in the game, between Moses Simon and Alex Iwobi. He said he threw up the decision to a vote between members of the technical crew. They voted slightly in favour of Moses Simon, hence Moses Simon started the game.
Before Alex Iwobi came unto the game, Coach Rohr told him on the side lines to try to score the winning goal for Nigeria!
When he came into the game, he did what Coach Rohr told him to do: he got the winning goal, in the 73rd minute of the game, off a pile driver of a shot, off a pass collected from right-back, Shehu Abdullahi!
The Super Eagles of Nigeria, thus, won the match, 1-0, and got the 2018 World cup ticket for Nigeria !!!!!!!!

IN THE AFTERMATH OF THE ENCOUNTER AGAINST THE ZAMBIANS
Nigerians cheered wildly with joy. The "Goodswil Akpabio International stadium," was turned into a carnival-like place. Nigerians were excited about another World cup adventure! It was indeed a pleasant feeling for Nigerians!
Coach Rohr, at a television sports programme, days after the match, was thanked profusely by the journalists who interviewed him, for making 180 million Nigerians happy, with the qualification for the 2018 World cup finals!
The author, in an article in the "Nigeria World Forum," titled : " The "nitty-gritty" Super Eagles of Nigeria, finally subdue the stubborn "Chipolopolo" and land in
Russia!,"(https://nigeriaworld.com/feature/publication/nwokeji/101717.html) and " The heroes of the 2018 World cup qualification,"(https://nigeriaworld.com/feature/publication/nwokeji/102417.html), paid tribute to the Super Eagles players, as well all the other stake holders who made qualification for the 2018 World cup possible.

NIGERIA VERSUS ALGERIA, 10th NOVEMBER, 2017.
The Super Eagles in the preparation for the last match of the 2018 World cup qualification series, against Algeria, had to cope with the absences of a number of players who couldn't come for the game, as a consequence of injuries. Players like: Elderson Echiejile, Simon Moses, Victor Moses, Odion Ighalo, Skipper John Mikel Obi and Ogenyi Onazi.
It was a weakened Super Eagles team that faced Algeria, in what was actually a dead rubber encounter, considering the fact the Super Eagles had already qualified for the World cup competition from the group!
The then Algerian coach, Rabah Madjer, who had just taken over coaching responsibility of the Algerian team, shortly before the Nigerian encounter, talked of how he didn't rate the Nigerian team highly. He said with the exception of Alex Iwobi, the other Nigerian players didn't play in the first team of their respective club sides. This in the author's candid opinion, was nothing but jealousy! The Super Eagles of Nigeria had proved themselves as winners of the qualifying group, to which Algeria belonged, in the race to the 2018 World cup competition!

The match took place in Constantine, on a bad pitch, that was barely playable. The Nigerian players had more difficulties playing on the pitch, this certainly affected their performance; and with benefit of hindsight, somehow contributed to robbing them of the deserved victory.

The following players played for Nigeria:

The goalkeeper was Ikechukwu Ezenwa.

The defenders were: Abdullahi Shehu, right- back; Ola Aina, left-back; William Troost-Ekong, centre-half back and Stand-in skipper Leon Balogun, left-half back.

The mid-fielders were: John Ogu, defensive mid-fielder; Wilfred Ndidi, defensive mid-fielder and Etebo Oghenekaro, offensive mid-fielder.

The attackers were: Kelechi Iheanacho, right winger; Alex Iwobi, left winger and Anthony Nwakaeme, who made his debut for Nigeria, centre-forward.

The Super Eagles played in a 4-3-3 formation.

The Super Eagles went on the offensive from the start of the match. They went after the Algerians, they were hungry for a win, notwithstanding the fact they had already qualified for the 2018 World cup tournament.

Apparently, Coach Rohr, wanted to end the qualification series with an out-right win against Algeria.

The Super Eagles controlled the game, had the better ball possession percentage, created some chances, but a combination of a poor playing surface and some measure of lack of clinical finishing robbed them of the deserved goals.

The Algerians were a much improved team, at least defensively, in comparison to the Algerian team that played the Super Eagles at the earlier stages of the 2018 World cup qualifying series, in 2016.

They put up a good fight against the Super Eagles, but still fell short of the standards of the Super Eagles of Nigeria.

The first half, ended, scoreless.

In the second half, both sides intensified the pace of their attacking soccer. However, the Nigerians got on the score sheet first: In the 66th minute, John Ogu, after collecting a loose ball midway into the Algerian territory, let go off a left-footed canon shot, that beat the Algerian goalkeeper hands down, as it flew into the top corner of the net, for Nigeria's first goal of the match!

The Algerians fought back, and pressurized the Super Eagles, looking for the equaliser. They could not find their way into the Nigerian vital area.

It looked as if they were going to suffer a home defeat, until in the 80th minute, when the Referee awarded a questionable penalty to the Algerians! The Algerians scored from the penalty, to equalise the match, 1-1.

The match, ended, 1-1.

The Super Eagles of Nigeria, thus, ended the qualification series without conceding a defeat!

THE DAY AFTER THE MATCH AGAINST THE ALGERIANS

The author appreciated the Super Eagles performance with an article in the "Nigeria World Forum" titled: "Nigeria 1, Algeria1: A dead rubber encounter!,"(https://nigeriaworld.com/feature/publication/nwokeji/111217.html)

There was a bombshell, that shook the Super Eagles camp and indeed all Nigerians: Defender Shehu Abdullahi, was ineligible to play against Algeria, as a consequence of two yellow cards he obtained earlier on, in the qualification series! This meant that Nigeria not only had to forfeit the point gained from the match, but as further punitive measure, was adjudged to have lost the match to Algeria, with a score of 3-0!

The critical question is: Suppose Nigeria hadn't gotten the World cup ticket, after the victory over the Zambians and needed the point(s) against Algeria to qualify, what would have happened in the event of fielding an ineligible player? Your guess is as good as the author's!

NIGERIA VERSUS ARGENTINA, 14th NOVEMBER, 2017.

The Super Eagles of Nigeria took on the "Albaceleste" of Argentina, in a friendly encounter in the Russian city of Krasnador. The Super Eagles were originally billed to take on Saudi-Arabia, in a friendly on the same date, but Coach Gernot Rohr preferred the Argentinians, whom he felt would give the Super Eagles a good run for their money and provide a better basis to assess the Super Eagles progress, then.

The Super Eagles on arrival in Krasnador, were joined by Skipper John Obi Mikel.

The match in Krasnador, also afforded Coach Rohr, the opportunity to try out some new Super Eagles players. As shall be discussed later on.

On that day, the following players lined-up for Nigeria:

Goalkeeper Daniel Akpeyi, was in goal.

The defence line featured: Shehu Abdullahi, right-back; Ola Aina, left-back; Chidozie Awaziem, right-half back; William Troost-Ekong, centre-half back and Leon Baogun, left-half back.

The mid-field featured: Wilfred Ndidi, defensive mid-field; John Ogu, defensive mid-field and Skipper John Obi Mikel, offensive mid-field.

The attackers were: Kelechi Iheanacho and Alex Iwobi.

The Super Eagles of Nigeria, played in an usual: 5-3-2 formation!

It was a defensive-oriented formation, aimed at coping with the vast array of talented Argentinian players!

It must be mentioned that in this match, the Argentinian super star: Lionel Messi, didn't feature.

The match kicked off and the Super Eagles came under pressure, no thanks to the superior ball possession of the Argentinians. They controlled the mid-field; while the Super Eagles tried to get them on the counter.

This superiority in mid-field, resulted in two goals for Argentina, in the first half, scored in the 27th and 36th minutes.

The Super Eagles replied with a 45th minute goal, off a well taken free-kick by Kelechi Iheanacho, to bring scores in the first half to 2-1, in favour of Argentina.

For the second half, Coach Rohr quickly analysed the situation, he apparently came to the conclusion that the Super Eagles didn't put up an optimal performance in the first half, and made the following changes: Goalkeeper Francis Uzoho, replaced the fumbling Goalkeepr Daniel Akpeyi, whose blunder cost Nigeria the first goal. It was goalkeeper Uzoho's debut match for the Super Eagles of Nigeria!
He replaced Shehu Abdullahi, with Tyronne Ebuehi, who also made his debut for Nigeria.
He replaced Ola Aina, with Bryan Idowu, who also played his first match for Nigeria's Super Eagles on that day.
These changes proved effective, as one saw a different face of the Super Eagles in the second half. The Super Eagles played better and scored three second half goals in the: 52nd, 53rd and 73rd minutes, by Alex Iwobi (he scored the second and fourth goals) and Bryan Idowu! To take a commanding 4-2 lead, in a match they initially appeared to be losing in the first half.
The Super Eagles, finally, won the match: 4-2; to record a famous win against a "Lionel Messi-less" Argentina!

THE AFTERMATH OF THE MATCH AGAINST THE ARGENTINIANS
Nigerians expectedly were happy! The author appreciated the Super Eagles' performance with an article written on the "Nigeria World Forum," titled: " Nigeria 4, Argentina2: A hope-giving friendly Indeed!,"(https://nigeriaworld.com/feature/publication/nwokeji/112317.html)
 Some Nigerians already started talking of a semi-final appearance for the Super Eagles at the 2018 World cup.
But Coach Rohr, being the experienced coach he is, cautioned Nigerians on the need to be humble, as this was a friendly game.
At the post-match press conference, when some foreign journalists tried to minimise Nigeria' victory, by pointing out the fact that Lionel Messi didn't play for Argentina; he replied that he also missed the services of his star player: Victor Moses!

THE 2018 WORLD CUP DRAW
When the 2018 World cup draw took place at the "State Kremlin Palace," in Moscow, Russia, on 1st December, 2017, with Nigeria grouped together with: Croatia, Iceland and Argentina; yours sincerely knew it wouldn't be easy for Nigeria! This was because of the pedigree of the opponents of the Super Eagles of Nigeria. In an article on the "Nigeria World forum" titled : " A tough World cup draw for the Super Eagles of Nigeria," yours sincerely chronicled his thoughts on the Super Eagles' world cup group,(https://nigeriaworld.com/feature/publication/nwokeji/120817.html).

NIGERIA VERSUS POLAND, 23rd MARCH, 2018.

The Super Eagles of Nigeria took on the Polish national team in Poland, to kick start their 2018 World cup preparations. It was a friendly match that took place on a cold day in Poland.

The Super Eagles skipper: John Obi Mikel, couldn't play the match because of work permit issues, in his then playing base - China!

The Polish with a detailed knowledge of the Nigerian team, set out to win before their home crowd. They played against a Nigerian team that had an inexperienced 19 year-old goalkeeper! Their aim was to 'break-up' the Nigerian team, capitalising on the inexperience of their young goalkeeper. The young goalkeeper, Francis Uzoho, was initially, nervous, and apparently, not equal to the task. But as time went on, he re-adjusted to the pressures of the match, and still put up a good performance.

Coach Gernot Rohr fielded the following players:

Goalkeeper Francis Uzoho, was in goal.

The defence line featured: Shehu Abdullahi, right-back; Bryan Idowu, left-back; Stand-in Skipper William Troost-Ekong, centre-half back and Leon Balogun, left-half back.

The mid-fielders were: Wilfred Ndidi, defensive mid-fielder; Joel Obi, central mid-fielder; Victor Moses, wing offensive mid-fielder and Alex Iwobi, wing offensive mid-fielder.

The attackers were: Kelechi Iheanacho, supporting striker and Odion Ighalo, deepest striker.

The Super Eagles played in a 4-4-2 formation.

And were subjected to an initial Polish attacking salvo, from the onset of the game. The Polish dominated the mid-field and occasionally created half chances, which they could not utilise.

The Super Eagles, occasionally, took the game to the Polish.

Towards the end of the first half, the Polish team scored what looked like a good goal, which was fortuitously disallowed by the referee!

The first half, ended, scoreless.

In the second half, the Polish team intensified their search for a goal. They continued dominating the game, with the Nigerians, occasionally, threatening them.

In the 60th minute, a brilliant solo run by Victor Moses, into the Polish penalty box, resulted in his being tripped by a Polish defender. The referee instantly called for a penalty kick against Poland. This was expertly converted by Victor Moses, for the lone goal of the match!

The Polish tried to come back by increasing the pressure on the Nigerians. However, the tactically erudite Coach Gernot Rohr, cleverly closed the game on them, by ensuring that four of his six substitutions, were of a defensive nature!

The Super Eagles of Nigeria won the match, their first meeting with a Polish team, 1-0, to kick start their 2018 World cup preparations on a bright note!

Nigerians were happy, and the author appreciated their efforts in an article on the "Nigeria World Forum", titled:" Nigeria 1, Poland 0 : Super Eagles of Nigeria eek out a win in far away Poland!,"

(https://nigeriaworld.com/feature/publication/nwokeji/032518.html)

NIGERIA VERSUS SERBIA, 27th MARCH, 2018.
At the "Hive Stadium," Barnet, London, on the aforementioned date, the Super Eagles of Nigeria, played the Serbian national team in a friendly geared towards preparing the Super Eagles for the 2018 World cup tournament.
The Super Eagles of Nigeria met a Serbian team trying to make up for the earlier lost friendly match to Morocco, four days earlier in Italy.
The Super Eagles lined-up the following players:
Goalkeeper Francis Uzoho, was in goal. The defenders were: Tyronne Ebuehi, right- back; Bryan Idowu, left-back; William Troost-Ekong, centre-half back and Chidozie Awaziem, left-half back.
The mid-fielders were: Stand-in Skipper Ogenyi Onazi, defensive mid-fielder; Wilfred Ndidi, defensive mid-fielder; Alex Iwobi, offensive mid-fielder; Joel Obi, central mid-fielder and Victor Moses, offensive mid-fielder.
The lone striker was: Ahmed Musa.
The Super Eagles played in a 4-5-1 formation!
They met a stuggy and well- organised Serbian team, that gave them a run for their money. They Super Eagles also hit back at the Serbians with nice combination soccer; but lacked the necessary creativity needed to break open the tight and compact Serbian defensive organisation.
The Serbians also had difficulties breaking down the Super Eagles defensive organisation; but nonetheless, scored what looked like a good goal in the 13th minute of play, but it was, luckily for the Nigerians, disallowed by the referee!
The interesting first half, ended scoreless.
In the second half, the Serbians somehow began to find openings in the Nigerian defensive organisation, apparently, because Coach Rohr, changed the Super Eagles formation from a more compact 4-5-1, to a more offensive- oriented 4-4-2, with the introduction of Odion Ighalo, a striker, in the place of Victor Moses. While the Super Eagles' defensive formation gradually crumbled, the Serbians continued playing like one solid block, defensively and offensively: a better organised team! The Super Eagles also continued having difficulties creating the necessary space in the Serbian defensive area. They lacked the necessary creative ability to make the decisive final pass, to liberate the attackers to make hay!
This scenario continued till the end of the game.
The Serbians who improved considerably in their offensive/creative play in the second half, while of course maintaining their solid defensive organisation, deservedly, won the match, by 2-0; through goals scored in the 67th and 80th minutes!
The author appreciated the match on the "Nigeria World forum," with an article titled: "The Revealing Super Eagles' defeat to the Serbians in London!"
(https://nigeriaworld.com/feature/publication/nwokeji/040618.html)

TACTICAL REFLECTIONS ON THE MATCH
The Super Eagles lacked creativity in mid-field ; a problem which with benefit of hindsight, was to bedevil them at the 2018 World cup tournament!

NIGERIA VERSUS DEMOCRATIC REPUBLIC OF CONGO, 28TH MAY, 2018.
The Super Eagles played a friendly match against the Democratic Republic of Congo, in Port-harcourt, Nigeria, shortly before leaving for Europe for the last leg of preparations for the 2018 World cup competition. The aim of the friendly match was partly to say a big farewell to the ever- supportive Super Eagles' fans before the departure of the Super Eagles to Europe for the World cup competition and also partly to try out some fringe players of the Super Eagles team.
The match ended in a 1-1 draw.
Yours sincerely chronicled his thoughts on the match with an article on the "Nigeria World forum," titled: "Super Eagles of Nigeria1, DRC1:A farewell friendly on the home front!"
(https://nigeriaworld.com/feature/publication/nwokeji/060118.html).

THE DAY AFTER THE MATCH
There were two noteworthy events that took place after the aforementioned match:
Firstly, Simon Moses, was ruled out of the World cup party following an injury sustained during training in Port-harcourt, preparatory to the match against the Democratic Republic of Congo;
Secondly, Coach Rohr, announced the reduction of the original list of thirty players to twenty-five, before the team's departure to England, for the first leg of their European preparation for the World cup competition.

NIGERIA VERSUS ENGLAND, 2ND JUNE, 2018.
The Super Eagles took on the English national team in London, England, in their second preparatory match before the 2018 World cup competition.
The match started on a false note for the Super Eagles, as they were out-played in all departments of the game by the English side. They easily fell behind by 0-2, at half time.
The timely intervention of Coach Rohr tactically in the second half with the necessary re-adjustments brought the Super Eagles back into the match.
They scored a consolation goal by Alex Iwobi, to bring scores to 2-1; and, thus, suffered a respectable defeat to England.
The author saw the match as a match with two faces for the Super Eagles of Nigeria: A bad first half and a much better second half.
The details of how the author saw the match are chronicled in the article on the Nigeria world forum titled:" The two faces of the Super Eagles of Nigeria against the English national team !"

URL: https://nigeriaworld.com/feature/publication/nwokeji/060518.html

THE DAY AFTER THE MATCH AGAINST ENGLAND
Coach Gernot Rohr, finally dropped the last two players from the Super Eagles World cup squad and reduced the number of players to the mandatory twenty-three players.
The last two players dropped were: Ola Aina and Mike Agu. There were no doubt promising players, whose time to be fully-fledged Super Eagles would come in the future. Coach Rohr expressed these sentiments to them before bidding them farewell from the Super Eagles team to the 2018 World cup competition!

NIGERIA VERSUS CZECH REPUBLIC, 6th JUNE, 2018.
The Super Eagles took on the Czech national team on the aforementioned date for their last friendly match before the 2018 World cup competition, in Rannersdorf, Austria.
The match was a highly tactical one considering Coach Rohr's approach to the game. He used a highly tactical 5-3-2 formation. Apparently, based on the experience with the English national team.
The Super Eagles were much better organised from the beginning compared to the match against England.
They contained the offensive Czech national team, but hardly created chances of their own.
The Super Eagles lost the match by the oddest of margins: 1-0.
My impressions on the match are expressed in details in the article on the "Nigeria world forum" titled :"Super Eagles of Nigeria lose by the oddest of margins to the Czechs"
URL: *https://nigeriaworld.com/feature/publication/nwokeji/o 61018.html*

THE DAY AFTER THE LAST FRIENDLY MATCH OF THE SUPER EAGLES FOR THE 2018 WORLD CUP COMPETITION

Nigerians were worried by the spate of unimpressive performances put up by the Super Eagles in their friendly matches, more especially against World class opposition.
The question on their minds was: Are these Eagles ready for the world come the 2018 World cup competition?
Yours sincerely as an experienced soccer analyst, wrote an article on the "Nigeria World forum" titled :" Fellow Nigerians, don't write off the Super Eagles just yet!"
URL: *https://nigeriaworld.com/feature/publication/nwokeji/o 61318.html*

In that article, yours sincerely predicted a positive World cup performance by the Super Eagles of Nigeria!

THE 2018 WORLD CUP TOURNAMENT
Before the 2018 World cup competition began, Coach Gernot Rohr, made public the list of the twenty-three players that would represent Nigeria at the tournament:
Goalkeepers:
 Francis Uzoho
 Ikechukwu Ezenwa
 Daniel Akpeyi

Defenders:
Shehu Abdullahi
Bryan Idowu
Tyronne Ebuehi
Elderson Echiejile
Kenneth Omeruo
William Troost-Ekong
Leon Balogun
Chidozie Awaziem

Mid-fielders:
Skipper Mikel Obi
Joel Obi
Ogenyi Onazi
Etebo Oghenekaro
Wilfred Ndidi
John Ogu

Attackers:
Odion Ighalo
Kelechi Iheanacho
Ahmed Musa
Simeon Okonkwo
Victor Moses
Alex Iwobi

Details of the Super Eagles' 2018 World cup list are in my article published in the " Nigerian World forum"

URL: *https://nigeriaworld.com/feature/publication/nwokeji/o61418.html*

The Super Eagles of Nigeria were grouped together with : Croatia, Iceland and Argentina. In what was a sort of "group of death".
Nigerians as usual had high expectations for the team. Many Nigerians expected a quarter-final appearance for the Super Eagles. Some even expected the Super Eagles to get to the semi-finals!

NIGERIA VERSUS CROATIA 16TH JUNE, 2018.

The Super Eagles of Nigeria took on the Croatian national team, on the aforementioned date in the "Kaliningrad stadium", Kaliningrad, in their 2018 World cup opener.

The Super Eagles fans in Nigeria and world- wide expected much from the Super Eagles in this match.

My Belgian neighbour who had just read a copy of my book:" Super Eagles of Nigeria: Pride of Africa", and was so enthralled by its contents, told me he expected a Nigerian victory in the match. Yours sincerely as consequence, was under extra pressure knowing the quality of Nigeria's opponents.

The tactically erudite Coach Gernot Rohr, had gotten before the match, all the information he needed to prosecute the match from his team of scouts world-wide.

When the Referee sounded the whistle for commencement of the match, the Super Eagles players were ready to take on the Croatians. The Super Eagles played in a 4-2-3-1 formation.

Goalkeeper Uzoho was in goal.

The defenders were: Shehu Abdullahi, right back; Brian Idowu, left back; William Troost-Ekong, Centre-half back and Leon Balogun, left-half back.

The two defensive mid-fielders were: Wilfred Ndidi and Etebo Oghenekaro.

The right-sided offensive mid-fielder, was Victor Moses; the central mid-fielder was Skipper John Mikel Obi and the left-sided mid-fielder was Alex Iwobi.

The lone striker was: Odion Ighalo.

The Croatians took the early initiative and subjected the Super Eagles to much pressure; dominating the mid-field play. They however could not create chances notwithstanding their superior ball possession. The Super Eagles held their stand till the 32nd minute, when through a Croatian corner- kick, the ball was mistakenly deviated into the Nigerian net by mid-fielder Etebo Oghenekaro, for Croatia's first goal!

The Super Eagles tried to react to this goal, but found the Croatian defensive wall difficult to crack.

The first half, ended, 1-0 in favour of the Croatians.

In the second half, the Nigerians came out smoking taking the game to the Croatians, but once again met a rock solid Croatian defensive line.

This scenario continued till the 71st minute, when the over-zealous Nigerian central defender: William Troost-Ekong, fouled a Croatian attacker in the penalty box of Nigeria.

The resultant penalty awarded the Croatians, was expertly converted for Croatia's second goal.

The match ended 2-0, in favour of the better team: the Croatian national team. They also got the concomitant three points. The Super Eagles of Nigeria, were left with no point after the opening group's game.

THE DAY AFTER THE MATCH

Nigerians were expectedly disappointed at the outcome of the match. They expected more from the Super Eagles. A Nigerian told the author, she thought the Super Eagles played with fear in their hearts. She thought they didn't take on the Croatians confidently. Yours truly certainly was in agreement, as one saw in the match, a Super Eagles team that strangely played without character!
Internationally, the commentaries were negative with regards the Super Eagles' performance.
 The famed Coach Jose Mourinho, expressed disappointment at the Super Eagles' performance. And specifically faulted Coach Rohr's decision to play Skipper John Obi Mikel as offensive mid-fielder; he thought the skipper would have done better as defensive mid-fielder.
The foregoing showed the Super Eagles were already walking tight ropes after the first match! And flirted with early elimination from the 2018 World cup competition.
Something urgent had to be done to avert the possibility of an early Super Eagles exit from the World cup competition.
Coach Rohr, was thus, under tremendous pressure to make improvements in the Super Eagles 2018 World cup fortune, starting with the next game against Iceland.

NIGERIA VERSUS ICELAND, 22ND OF JUNE, 2018.
The Super Eagles of Nigeria, were given the foregoing, under tremendous pressure to do well against Iceland and, thus, rescue there now under threat World cup adventure.
Coach Rohr, was certainly under pressure and reacted by making the necessary changes to the team that lost to Croatia.
The Super Eagles lined-up thus, in their 3-5-2 formation:
Goalkeeper Francis Uzoho, was in goal.
The three central defenders were: Leon Balogun, right-half back; William Troost-Ekong, centre-half back and Kenneth Omeruo, left-half back.
The five-man mid-field had three defensive midfielders: Wilfred Ndidi, right-sided defensive mid-fielder; Ogenekharo Etebo, left-sided defensive mid-fielder and Skipper John Obi Mikel, central defensive/ - offensive mid-fielder.
Victor Moses, right-sided offensive mid-fielder and Brian Idowu, left-sided offensive mid-fielder.
The two-man attacking duo were Kelechi Iheanacho and Ahmed Musa.
Coach Rohr, thus, made three changes from the team that played Croatia.
He also changed the team's formation, from 4-2-3-1, to 3-5-2.
Coach Rohr, thus, responded completely to the opinion of the critics of the Super Eagles' first performance against Croatia. He used a formation that made the defensive, mid-field and offensive lines closer to each other.
And, thus, eliminated the yawning spaces between these lines in the match against Croatia, a tactical deficiency which the Croatians maximally exploited!
The Super Eagles, thus, played in a much more compact formation and played better from the beginning of the match.

We saw a much more confident-playing Super Eagles, who tried to take the game to their opponents. They, however, met an equally stuggy and compact-playing Icelanders who were also determined to win the game. Consequently, chances were not created in the first half; and the first half logically, ended, scoreless.

At half time, the highly expectant and – demanding fans of the Super Eagles of Nigeria, were angry, at what they described as a lack-lustre offensive display by the Super Eagles, in the first half; in which as it were, no single shot was fired at the Icelander's goal!!!

In the second half, the tactically erudite Coach Rohr, brought in the highly skilful, overlapping full-back: Tyronne Ebuehi, as a way of shoring –up the offensive display of the Super Eagles. Tyronne Ebuehi, played as a left-sided wide offensive mid-fielder. Coach exploited Tyronne Ebuehi's superb overlapping qualities to shore-up the Super Eagles' offensive thrusts. This worked out well as the Super Eagles turned the heat on the Icelanders in the second half; this coupled with their superior skills, made life a hell for the Icelanders in the second half. The Super Eagles scored in the 49th minute of the second half, off a brilliantly lobbed pass from Victor Moses to Ahmed Musa, which was expertly controlled by the latter, to fire home from close range, Nigeria's first goal! The score of Nigeria1, Iceland 0, was relieving to Nigerians!

The Super Eagles piled on more pressure, and were rewarded in the 75th minute by a second Ahmed Musa goal off a brilliant solo effort, after latching on to a Kenneth Omeruo's clearance. With scores, Nigeria 2, Iceland 0, the game was as good as played ; until the 83rd minute, when a defensive indiscretion by Tyronne Ebuehi, resulted in a penalty award to the Icelanders, which they failed to utilise!

The game ended in favour of Nigeria. And the Super Eagles' chances once again looked bright!

THE DAY AFTER THE GAME AGAINST ICELAND

The ecstatic Nigerians while savouring the sweet victory over the Icelanders, were nonetheless wary of the Super Eagles' next opponents: the "Albaceleste" of Argentina. Given the World cup record of both teams confrontations, Nigerians knew that to qualify from the group, which would entail at least a draw against Argentina, they would be at their utmost best against an Argentinian team that needed to win to qualify.

Apparently, given this reality, the Nigerians were somewhat subdued in their excitement over the victory over Iceland!

NIGERIA VERSUS ARGENTINA, 26TH JUNE 2018.

A Nigerian friend of the author's one met a day before the match-up with Argentina, told me, he expected a hell of a fight from the Argentinians, since in his own words: they would come all out to defeat the Super Eagles of Nigeria, to qualify for the next round of the World cup competition!

However, as an unrepentant Super Eagles enthusiast, yours sincerely hoped for victory, and wrote an article in the www. Nigeriaworld . com forum, in which one expressed hope in the eventual qualification of the Super Eagles for the second round of the World cup competition, notwithstanding the likely obstacle to be posed by the Argentinians! : "Why the Super Eagles of Nigeria, must, please God, defeat the Argentinian national team, come the 26th of June 2018."

URL: *https://nigeriaworld.com/feature/publication/nwokeji/o62518.html*

 Coach Rohr used the same team that started against Iceland against Argentina: You don't change a winning team! He also used the same tactics: 3-5-2.
The match started with the Argentinians dictating the pace of the game. They scored early in the 14th minute, through the geniality of Skipper Lionel Messi. He capitalised on an apparent loss of concentration on the part of the Super Eagles defenders to make hay.
The Argentinians kept on coming and came close to scoring on a number of occasions.
The first half, ended, 1-0, in favour of the Argentinians.
In the second half, the Super Eagles, apparently, rejuvenated by the halftime pep talk of Coach Rohr, came out smoking; and took the game to their opponents. They were adequately rewarded with a 51st minute penalty, after a foul on Leon Balogun, in the Argentinian penalty box, during a Nigerian corner kick. The resultant penalty kick was expertly converted by Victor Moses, to give Nigeria, a deserved 1-1 score line.
The rest of the minutes of the game that was played, was for yours sincerely a time- watching event; as yours sincerely focused a lot on the clock, that one wished could tick away faster, as a drawn game would favour the Super Eagles of Nigeria!
However, it was not to be, as the Argentinians, scored an 86th minute winner, to bring scores to 2-1; and secure qualification for the second round of the competition.
The Super Eagles of Nigeria, were thus, eliminated from the 2018 World cup competition, in the preliminary rounds!

THE AFTERMATH OF NIGERIA'S EARLY ELIMINATION FROM THE 2018 WORLD CUP TOURNAMENT.
Nigerians were somewhat disappointed at an unexpected early elimination from the 2018 World cup competition. But, however, tempered their disappointment by the realisation that the team was a young team. As a matter of fact, the team had the lowest average age of all the teams that were at the 2018 World cup competition! Nigerians correctly saw the team as a team of the future; for whom the 2018 World cup competition came way too early! Thus, nobody called for the head of Coach Gernot Rohr!

However, as a rather unfortunate footnote in the 2018 Super Eagles world cup story, striker Odion Ighalo was hounded by some fanatic Super Eagles fans for the miss he recorded in front of the Argentinian goal, in the Super Eagles' final encounter at the World cup competition. Odion Ighalo, has since shaken off that disappointment to become even a much more deadly striker!

POST MORTEM ANALYSIS THE COACH GERNOT ROHR'S ERA
Coach Gernot Rohr's era as at the time of writing is still ongoing. Thus, it would be unconventional to write a post-mortem analysis of a coach who still has contract with the Super Eagles of Nigeria. That would be done at a later date.

CHAPTER 9

THE LEGENDARY SOCCER COMMENTATOR: FABIO LANIPEKUN
Mr. Fabio Lanipekun, was a soccer commentator in the mould of the also legendary soccer commentator, the late Earnest Okonkwo, of blessed memory. He helped revolutionise soccer commentary in Nigeria. He brought vivid descriptions of soccer events in a way that gave the listener the impression the listener was watching the match live.
He was a very thorough broadcaster, who loved his job and gave it his very best. He was not only a good broadcaster/commentator, he was also a good discoverer of soccer talent. Some of the Nigerian players of yore who went on to become great stars, were earlier on recognised by him as potentially good players, with great future in the game.
He was a patriotic Nigerian, who not only commented on the Super Eagles' matches as well as matches involving other Nigerian soccer sides, but was actively involved in their evolutionary process, by dutifully serving in committees set up to improve their performance. Needless saying that at those committee meetings, his contributions were of immeasurable importance and helped shape the destiny of Nigerian teams in a positive way!
He has certainly left his indelible footprints in the immeasurable soccer sands of time! The Nigerian nation will for ever be grateful to him for his efforts at having helped raise soccer to what it is today in Nigeria: a 'religion' of sorts that acts as a great unifier for Nigerians!!!! He will go down in history as one of the best soccer commentators ever to have come out of Nigeria, nay Africa!
Yours sincerely wishes him well, in his future life's endeavours! May his shadow never grow less! Iseeeeeeeehhhh!!!!!!!!

CHAPTER 10

GENERAL CONCLUSIONS

The reality of Super Eagles of Nigeria in the new Era, is that a lot of expectations have been placed on the Super Eagles of Nigeria, by the highly demanding Nigerian fans. The team no doubt has come a long way, in it's evolutionary process. The team no doubt has made remarkable progress in it's evolution thus far: Winning three African Nations' cup titles; Qualifying six times for the FIFA World cup competition and has also attained Africa's highest rating so far at the FIFA rankings for national teams: the fifth best team in the world in 1994!

One must confess the Super Eagles performance over the years have been epileptic. This lack of consistency on the part of the team, can be easily adduced to the epileptic style of soccer administration in Nigeria. In order words, Nigeria has had NFF – Nigerian Football Federation- administrations that have been inconsistent in the administration of soccer over the years. Some NFF administrations virtually 'kill' soccer in Nigeria, before other NFF administrations attempt to 'resurrect' it. These inconsistencies in soccer administration, as earlier stated, affects the Super Eagles' fortunes negatively. The lacuna created as a consequence of NFF's inconsistent soccer management style, always gives other more organised soccer nations a huge advantage over Nigeria. They always appear to be one or some steps ahead of Nigeria!

An example, is the 1994 Super Eagles World cup squad, that was then rated the fifth best team of the world! They played beautiful soccer at the 1994 World cup tournament ; and was adjudged by experts as being rich in talent! Under more decent soccer climes, that team would have been consistently given the best circumstances to develop to greater heights. As a matter of fact, soccer commentators who saw the team's performance at the 1994 World cup tournament, coupled with Nigeria's Olympic-winning performance in 1996, came to the conclusion that Nigeria would get to at least the semi-finals of the 1998 World cup tournament. But that was not the case, as the Super Eagles underperformed! The reason was not far-fetched: inconsistent soccer administration!!!! The 'capital' gained from the 1994 World cup performance was squandered on the altar of inconsistent and ineffective NFF administration!

This has been the story with the evolution of the Super Eagles over the years. As a consequence, the Super Eagles of Nigeria, have failed to reach the heights they are supposed to get to given their potentialities. They have failed to meet the ultimate expectations of Nigerians. As earlier stated, some progress has been made, but more could still done.

If a country like Greece, with certainly not as much talents as Nigeria, could win the European Championships, in 2004, ten years after they were defeated by Nigeria, by the wonderful Super Eagles of the 1994 World cup tournament; a country like Nigeria with her array of talents under normal circumstances, should have won or at least played the final of a FIFA World cup competition !!!!!

In order words, the Super Eagles, notwithstanding some successes, have failed to reach the required heights given their potentials, for earlier stated reasons.

The critical question at this juncture is: Is the situation of the Super Eagles hopeless, with regards expectations of Nigerians? The answer is: No, certainly not. The Super Eagles given their attributes and given the attributes/potentials of Nigeria, can still get to the summit of their potentials; as long as a consistently effective, functional and pro-active NFF, takes charge of it's affairs!

UP SUPER EAGLES ! UP NIGERIA !!!!!!!!!!

REFERENCES
1) Personal knowledge and experience.
2) For review of certain matches played by Nigeria:
   https://www.youtube.com/

THANKS AND APPRECIATIONS

The author's utmost gratitude is to his family for the usual support given for this project.
The author, is also greatly indebted to friends and well-wishers who encouraged him in carrying out this project.
Most importantly, the author's profoundest gratitude is to God Almighty for his consistent and benevolent guidance and most importantly for imbuing me with talent without which this project wouldn't be realised! To him I will be eternally grateful for his consistent and benevolent blessings on me and my family.

TO ALMIGHTY GOD BE THE GLORY !!!!!!!!!